SEARCH ENGINE OPTIMIZATION

Backlinking for SEO: 110% Complete Guide for Backlinks SEO to get 80+ DA in 2020

A perfect book to grow your domain 1000% DA and PA. Boost your organic traffic 110% and get geo-targeted traffic. This is a complete book for SEO Agencies and Affiliate Marketers.

Umair Ahmad

Table Of Contents

What are backlinks?   6

Why are backlinks important?   6

   How to Get Backlinks?   7

Earning and giving backlinks   8

Competitive backlink research   8

What is: Backlink   9

   How Do Backlinks Work?   9

   Types of Backlinks   10

   How Can I Check My Backlinks?   10

WHAT ARE BACKLINKS IN SEO AND WHAT ARE THE   13
ADVANTAGES OF BACKLINKS?

Advantages of backlinks in SEO: 14

   1. Improves Organic Ranking   15

   2. Faster Indexing   16

   3. Referral Traffic   16

How to start getting backlinks: 16

   1. Write awesome articles   17

   2. Start guest blogging   18

   3. Replicate your competitors' backlinks   20

   4. Broken link building   22

   5. Submit to web directories   23

What Are Backlinks?   24

Why Are Backlinks Important?   24

What Types of Backlinks are Valuable?   27

Trait #1: They Come From Trusted, Authoritative   27
Websites

Trait #2: They Include Your Target Keyword In The   29
Link's Anchor Text

Trait #3: The Site (and Page) Linking to You Is   30

Topically Related To Your Site

Trait #4: The Link Is a "Dofollow" Link   31

Trait #5: The Link Is From a Domain That Hasn't   31
Linked to You Before

Best Practices   33

Create a Linkable Assets   33

Build Backlinks from Link Roundups   37

Use The Moving Man Method   39

Broken Link Building   41

Guest Posting   43

Infographics and Other Visual Assets   46

Submit Testimonials   49

Blogger Reviews   50

Link Reclamation   52

Use HARO   54

Reverse Engineer Your Competitor's Backlinks   56

Stick to Content Formats That Generate Links   57

10 Smart Ways to Earn or Build Backlinks to Your   59
Website

1. The broken-link building method   59

2. Backlinks through infographics   60

3. The advantage of guest articles   61

4. Spy on your competitors.   64

5. Build internal links.   65

6. Promote your content.   65

7. Write testimonials.   66

8. Contact journalists and important bloggers.   67

9. Donate.   69

10. Get interviewed.   69

Conclusion   69

How to Build Backlinks in 2020 (NEW Guide)   70

What are Backlinks (and How Do They Work)?   70

When to Build Backlinks   71

1. Fix All Technical/UX Issues 72

Redirect Chains 72

302s 73

Reclaim Lost Link Juice (404 Link Reclamation) 73

Fix Broken External Links 74

2. Develop a Strong Site Architecture 74

3. Create Linkable Assets 75

7 Backlink Quality Indicators 76

1. Relevance 76

The Relevancy Pyramid 76

Tier One: 100% Relevancy 77

Tier Two: 75% Relevancy 77

Tier Three: 50% Relevancy 77

Tier Four: 25% Relevancy 77

Tier Five: 0% Relevancy 77

Local Relevancy Pyramid 80

Tier One: 100% Geo-Targeted and Niche Relevant 80

Tier Two: 100% Niche Relevant 80

Tier Three: 100% Geo-Targeted 80

Tier Four: 50% Niche Relevant 80

Tier Five: 25% Niche Relevant 81

2. Authority 82

3. Link Quality 82

4. Traffic 82

5. Editorial Standards 83

6. Outbound Link Quality 83

7. Indexation 83

Harmful Backlinks to AVOID 84

(Almost) Everything That's Irrelevant 84

Public Networks 84

Automated Backlinks 86

How to Build "Foundational" Backlinks 86

Business Listings/Citations 87

Niche-Targeted Directories 87

Geo-Targeted Directories 88

Niche Relevant Forum Backlinks 90

1. Prospect for relevant forums 90

2. Take time to fill out your profile 90

3. Understand the forum "personality" / etiquette 91

4. Increase your post count & start adding friends 91

5. Start a thread 91

Power Backlinks 91

Content-Driven Approach 92

Editorial Backlinks 92

Niche Relevant Guest Posts 93

The Merger Technique 93

Resource Pages 94

The White Alternative to PBNs 94

Grey Hat Backlinks 95

Leverage Relevant Expired Domains 95

Web 2.0s 96

How to EARN Backlinks 96

11 Ways to Earn Backlinks 97

1. You Have to Become User-Centric 97

2. Your Content Must Please the User 99

3. Your Content Stand Outs 101

Outdated Content 102

Lack of Depth 103

Lack of Data or Research 103

Lack of Personality 103

Lack of Readability & Visual Appeal 104

4. You Must Be Willing to Do What Others Won't 105

5. You Must Be Creative 105

7. You Must Outperform Others   106

8. You Have to Be Consistent   107

9. You Have to Build Relationships   108

10. You Need to Build an Email List   110

11. You Need to Promote Your Content   110

Similar Content Outreach   111

Bonus: What About Guest Posting?   111

Frequently Asked Questions About Backlinks   112

My backlinks are decreasing. What now?   112

My backlinks are not showing in Google Search Console, Ahrefs, etc. Why?   112

Are backlinks still important?   112

Are Fiverr backlinks good?   112

Are NoFollow backlinks good?   113

How many backlinks do I need?   113

How many backlinks per day is safe?   113

How many backlinks do I have?   113

That's a Wrap!   113

About Author

Umair Ahmad

Umair Ahmad is a Founder & CEO at Youth Group Limited. By profession, he is a Software Engineer. He has another title linked with his name that is world Youngest Peace Promoter. He is also a Young Entrepreneur. Youth Group Limited, Youth Academy, Youth Institute of Technology, Google Gang, USoft FM Radio, The Youth and Youth HD TV are some well- known foundation by him. He is also from the board of directors at Iftikhar Traders. As a Founder and CEO of Youth Group Limited Umair's reforms are amazing. Early Life Umair Ahmad born (16 April 1997) at Lahore, Punjab, Pakistan, his father name is Iftikhar Ahmad Butt, Umair was a simple, neat and clean boy in his Childhood. On Umair's birthday his grand-father see a dream a "SUN is rising on the top of their house, and with his brightness everything of their house is Glowing". From his early life, he has no interest in the dramatic educational system of this world. He always wants to learn skills and do things practically. But his family want something else that was fully against the nature of Umair Ahmad. So, as a student, he was a week student, and still now at his young age. His views are the same as he has in past. Career Founder Youth Group Limited Youth Academy Youth Institute of Technology Youth HD TV USoft FM Radio Pakistan Learning Point University of Youth The Youth (Online Newspaper) Co-Founder MaOS.PK (Online e-Commerce Store)

What are backlinks?

Backlinks, also called "inbound links" or "incoming links," are created when one website links to another. The link to an external website is called a *backlink.*

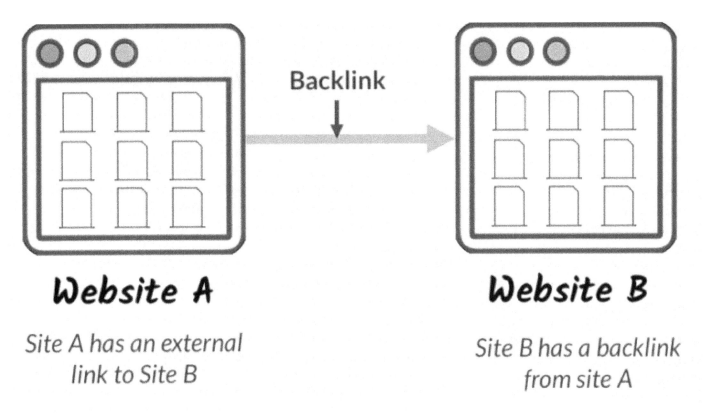

Website A

Site A has an external link to Site B

Website B

Site B has a backlink from site A

Why are backlinks important?

Backlinks are especially valuable for SEO because they represent a "vote of confidence" from one site to another.

In essence, backlinks to your website are a signal to search engines that others vouch for your content. If many sites link to the same webpage or website, search engines can infer that content is worth linking to, and therefore also worth surfacing on a SERP. So, earning these backlinks can have a positive effect on a site's ranking position or search visibility.

There are two basic types of backlinks, and one is more valuable than the other. Let's take a quick look at each one and how they affect your site.

Nofollow Backlink

```
<a href="https://yoursite.com/blog" rel="nofollow">
```

Dofollow Backlink

```
<a href="https://yoursite.com/blog" >
```

A Nofollow tag tells search engines to ignore a link. They don't pass any value from one site to another. So, typically they aren't helpful in improving your search rank or visibility.

Dofollow links are the type of backlink that everyone wants. Just keep in mind that those coming from respected sites hold the most value. This kind of backlink can help improve your search engine rankings.

However, there are dofollow links that are considered being bad or 'toxic'. These links come from suspicious sites or are gained by breaking the search engine terms of service.

This may cause Google to penalize or even de-index your site. Remember, it's not about the quantity of backlinks, but rather the quality that makes the difference in ranking.

How to Get Backlinks?

Building backlinks to your site takes time and effort. Here are 7 simple ways you can start building quality backlinks for your website.

Earning and giving backlinks

Earning backlinks is an essential component of off-site SEO. The process of obtaining these links is known as link earning or link building.

Some backlinks are inherently more valuable than others. Followed backlinks from trustworthy, popular, high-authority sites are considered the most desirable backlinks to earn, while backlinks from low-authority, potentially spammy sites are typically at the other end of the spectrum. Whether or not a link is followed (i.e. whether a site owner specifically instructs search engines to pass, or not pass, link equity) is certainly relevant, but don't entirely discount the value of nofollow links. Even just being mentioned on high-quality websites can give your brand a boost.

Just as some backlinks you earn are more valuable than others, links you create to other sites also differ in value. When linking out to an external site, the choices you make regarding the page from which you link (its page authority, content, search engine accessibility, and so on) the anchor text you use, whether you choose to follow or nofollow the link, and any other meta tags associated with the linking page can have a heavy impact on the value you confer.

Competitive backlink research

Backlinks can be time-consuming to earn. New sites or those expanding their keyword footprint may find it difficult to know where to start when it comes to link building. That's where competitive backlink research comes in: By examining the backlink profile (the collection of pages and domains linking to a website) to a competitor that's already ranking well for your target keywords, you can gain insight about the link building that may have helped them. A backlink tool like Link Explorer can help uncover these links so you can and target those domains in your own link building campaigns.

What is: Backlink

A backlink is simply a link from one website to another. Search engines like Google use backlink as a ranking signal because when one website links to another, it means they believe the content is noteworthy. High-quality backlinks can help to increase a site's ranking position and visibility in search engine results (SEO).

WHAT IS:

Backlink

(EXPLAINED)

How Do Backlinks Work?

Backlinks play an important role in search engine algorithm, SEO, and your overall strategy for growing your website.

The easiest way to think of backlinks would be as conversations among websites.

For example, John is a blogger, and he writes a very interesting article about a sports event.

Another blogger, Samantha, links to John's article when sharing her perspective. Since she writes about the topic on her well-known online magazine site, this creates a backlink to John's post.

Because the online magazine is popular, many other sites will link back to her article. This increases the online magazine's authority, and John's article also gets a valuable backlink from a reputable site.

Basically it's a win-

win. Types of

Backlinks

- Add links to your site on your social media profiles.
- Do a Google search for a post that's already ranking well and then improve and expand it.
- Create list posts, "how-to" posts, "why" posts, infographics, or posts with embedded videos. These formats usually get more backlinks than standard posts.
- Write the ultimate guide posts. These are very long posts containing several thousand words and cover every angle of the topic.
- Write guest posts on other blogs and websites
- Contact influencers in your niche or industry and tell them about an article on your site that they may want to link to.
- Interview influencers in your industry and send them a link, no doubt they will link back to your site.

You can also begin doing competitive backlink research. In order to do this, you'll need to see the backlinks of your competitors who are ranking well.

A backlink tool like SEMrush can help you find these links, so you can begin targeting those domains as part of your own link building strategy.

How Can I Check My Backlinks?

There are various backlink monitoring tools that let you check your website backlinks including Google Search Console, SEMRush, Ahrefs, etc.

Keeping an eye on your backlinks is very important. Google Webmaster Guidelines require you to ask toxic website owners to remove their links from your site. If you don't, then Google can penalize your website, and your page rank will begin to drop in search results.

So, it's important to know how to answer these 3 questions:

- Where can I find all my
- backlinks? How can I know if
  they are toxic?
- How can I contact toxic backlink site owners?

Thankfully, the answer is easy with the right tools.

You can use Google Search Console to help grow your site and see your backlinks, but it can take a lot of time and it's limited on what it can do.

However, there are faster and better tools available. For example, by using SEMrush, you can quickly answer all three of those important questions and much more.

SEMrush has two main areas that deal specifically with backlinks. The first is the Backlink Analytics section which lets you study your competitors, and the second is the Backlink Audit area.

Let's take a quick look at Backlink Audit section because it lets you find all the backlinks to your site.

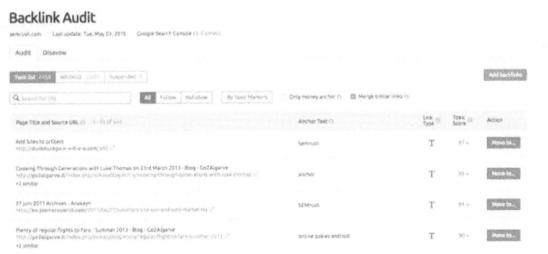

Next, SEMrush's Backlink Audit tool checks every backlink and sorts out those that are toxic. This way you can find and disavow toxic backlinks before Google penalizes your website.

And one of the best things about SEMrush is it lets you email the toxic website owner right from the user screen.

With a tool like SEMrush, you can do keyword research, see your competitors backlinks, and manage yours in one convenient place.

Keeping track of your backlink profile will tell you a lot about the value of your site and is an important part of your site's SEO strategy.

We hope this guide helped you learn what are backlinks, and how you can use them to grow your website.

WHAT ARE BACKLINKS IN SEO AND WHAT ARE THE ADVANTAGES OF BACKLINKS?

A "backlink" is one of the most used words in the world of search engine optimization (SEO).

Many bloggers who have only recently started a blog or a website often struggle to understand what the term "backlink" means.

In this post, I hope to offer you an understanding of what backlinks are, why they are essential to SEO, and why they are important for your online success. You'll also learn how to analyze the backlinks of your competitors, and how to acquire them for your site.

Let's get started…

Backlinks are incoming links to a webpage.

When a webpage links to any other page, it's called a backlink. In the past, backlinks were the major metric for the ranking of a webpage. A page with a lot of backlinks tended to rank higher on all major search engines, including Google. This is still true to a large extent.

Here is a glossary of common terms related to backlinks that you should know:

- **Link Juice**: When a webpage links to any of your articles or your website's homepage, it passes "link juice". This link juice helps with the ranking of the article, and also improves the domain authority. As a blogger, you can stop passing link juice by using a no-follow tag.
- **No-Follow Link**: When a website links to another website, but the link has a no-follow tag, that link does not pass link juice. No-follow links are not useful concerning the ranking of a page as they do not contribute anything. In general, a webmaster uses the no-follow tag when he/she is linking out to an unreliable site. **Do-Follow Link**: By default, all the links that you add to a blog post are do-follow links and these pass link juice.
- **Linking Root Domains**: This refers to the number of backlinks coming into your website from a unique domain. Even if a website has linked to your website ten times, it will only be considered as *one* linked root domain.
- **Low-Quality Links**: Low-quality links are links that come from harvested sites, automated sites, spam sites, or even porn sites. Such links do far more harm than good. This is one reason you should be careful when buying backlinks.
- **Internal Links**: Links that are going from one page to another within the same domain are called internal links. The process itself is referred to as *internal linking* or *interlinking.*
- **Anchor Text**: Text that is used for hyperlinks is called anchor text. Anchor text backlinks work great when you are trying to rank for particular keywords.

Advantages of backlinks in SEO:

Before I talk about the advantages of backlinks, you need to know that much has changed concerning backlinks in the past couple of years.

There was a time when even low-quality links helped in ranking a site. But ever since Google rolled out its Penguin algorithm, the whole landscape of backlinking has changed.

It is important to have backlinks from quality sites, and those backlinks should be contextual. If, for example, you have a site about fish, and you are creating links from other niche sites about monkeys, these links will be of no use. Your goal should be to get links from authoritative and relevant sites.

Now let's take a look at why it is important for you to create backlinks to your site:

1. Improves Organic Ranking

Backlinks help in getting better search engine rankings.

Important note: "SERP" means search engine results page. This screenshot is merely reflecting what people see in Google.

Here's an example.

Take the topic "SEO Backlinks".

If I enter this search term into Ahrefs' Keywords Explorer (a keyword research tool), I can see that most of the high-ranking pages have tons of backlinks:

If your content is getting links from other sites, that content will naturally start to rank higher in the search results. If it isn't, then you need to get proactive and build them.

Your goal should be to create links to individual posts/pages along with those leading to your homepage.

2. Faster Indexing

Search engine bots discover new webpages by following backlinks from existing webpages. Only when they've discovered your site can they crawl your site effectively.

It will be more difficult for search engine bots to find your site if you do not have any backlinks. Especially for a new website, it is important to get backlinks as they help in the faster discovery and indexing of your site.

3. Referral Traffic

One of the major benefits of backlinks is that they help get referral traffic. Basically, a person who is reading a post may click on links in the post to find out more about the topic at hand.

Since people click on links voluntarily, they're usually more targeted and are less likely to leave the page fast (aka a low bounce rate).

Usually, referral traffic is targeted and has a low bounce

rate. Learn:

What is anchor text and what is the SEO importance of anchored text?

How to start getting backlinks:

So now you understand what the term "backlink" means as it relates to SEO and why they're important. Let's now learn a few simple techniques for acquiring new backlinks:

One important fact that you need to keep in mind about backlink SEO is that it is not the *number of backlinks* which matters, but rather the **quality of backlinks.**

If you are using some paid services to get links to your site, you are likely going to be penalized by Google Penguin's algorithm.

So here's the question:

What are some of the ways to get *quality* backlinks for your blog?

1. Write awesome articles
2. Use Broken link building method
3. Replicating your competitors' backlinks
4. Create cornerstone articles (Piller articles)
5. Start guest blogging
6. Submit to web directories

1. Write awesome articles

If you want people to link to you, you need to give them a reason. And the best reason is an awesome article.

If your content is helpful and enjoyable, people will be happy to link to

it. How do you create an awesome article?

Here are some tips to get you started:

- Solve the problem. Most people read content because they're looking for a solution. Make sure you articulate the exact problem and teach them how to fix it.
- Make your content easy to read. Write it in short, simple sentences. Make the article look less chunky by adding formatting, headings, images and other multimedia.
- Have a unique angle. There's so much content on the Internet today. How will your article stand out?
- Build authority into the article. People want to learn from people with authority on that topic. If you're not one, you can always interview and quote experts.

Over the years, we've published plenty of articles on this blog that will help you to create great articles in no time:

- SEO Copywriting Tips (Write SEO Optimized content)
- On Page SEO Techniques (This is highly recommended)
- Five Writing Tips To Connect With Readers At A Deeper Level

Once you've published your awesome post, it's time to send some outreach emails. A good group of people to reach out to are those who have published articles on the same topic. Since they've written on that topic before, there is a higher probability that they'll be interested in seeing your post.

To find these people, simply enter the topic of your article (remember to try variations!) into Google. Collect the list of articles that appear in the SERPs.

Alternatively, you can use a tool like BuzzSumo.

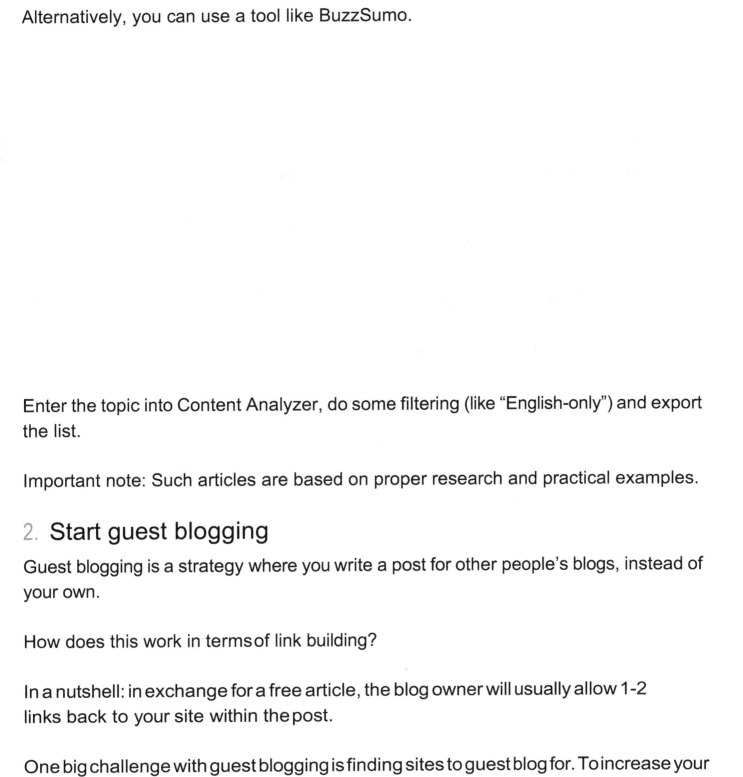

Enter the topic into Content Analyzer, do some filtering (like "English-only") and export the list.

Important note: Such articles are based on proper research and practical examples.

2. Start guest blogging

Guest blogging is a strategy where you write a post for other people's blogs, instead of your own.

How does this work in terms of link building?

In a nutshell: in exchange for a free article, the blog owner will usually allow 1-2 links back to your site within the post.

One big challenge with guest blogging is finding sites to guest blog for. To increase your chances of being accepted, you can look for sites that are already accepting guest posts. These sites typically have a page calling for contributors, like a "Write For Us" or "Contribute" page. To find these sites, you can use Google's advanced search operators.

Some search operators you can use:

- [your_topic] "write for us"
- [your_topic] "become an
- author" [your_topic] "guest
- post" [your_topic] "guest
- article" [your_topic]
  inurl:contribute

From there, simply follow the instructions and submit a pitch.

Another route you can take is to look for guest blogging opportunities in Ahrefs' Content Explorer.

The reason is this: if a website has written about a topic before, they clearly have an interest in it. Thus, they may be willing to accept a guest post about that topic, even if they don't have a "write for us" page.

To begin, enter any word/phrase in your niche.

Check the "one article per domain" box to get a list of unique domains you can potentially write for. You can also add a few more filters to narrow the list so you can pitch blogs you're comfortable writing for.

Some of these sites may not have an obvious "Write for us" page. Nevertheless, most blogs will accept a guest post if your pitch or topic is good enough.

One way to find good topics to pitch is to note common themes or topics that are already popular on their blog.

Most blogs showcase their best articles on their site.

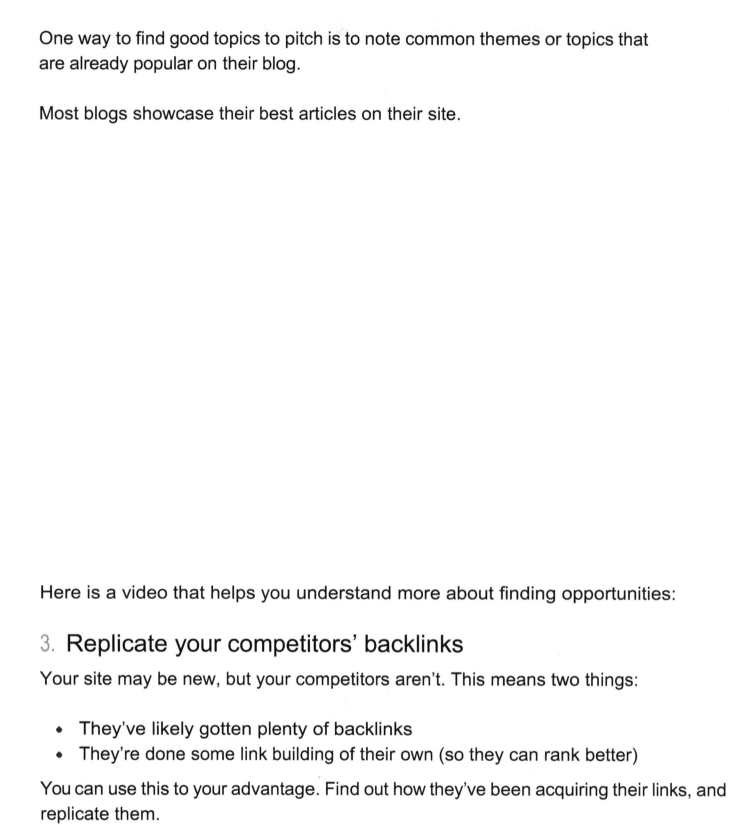

Here is a video that helps you understand more about finding opportunities:

3. Replicate your competitors' backlinks

Your site may be new, but your competitors aren't. This means two things:

- They've likely gotten plenty of backlinks
- They're done some link building of their own (so they can rank better)

You can use this to your advantage. Find out how they've been acquiring their links, and replicate them.

To do this, you'll have to use a tool in Ahrefs called Link Intersect. This handy tool tells you who's linking to multiple competitors, but not to you.

In the below screenshot, you can see there are about 48,000 domains that are linking to my closest competitors. What I'll do is to analyze the results and figure out why they linked to my competitors, but not to me.

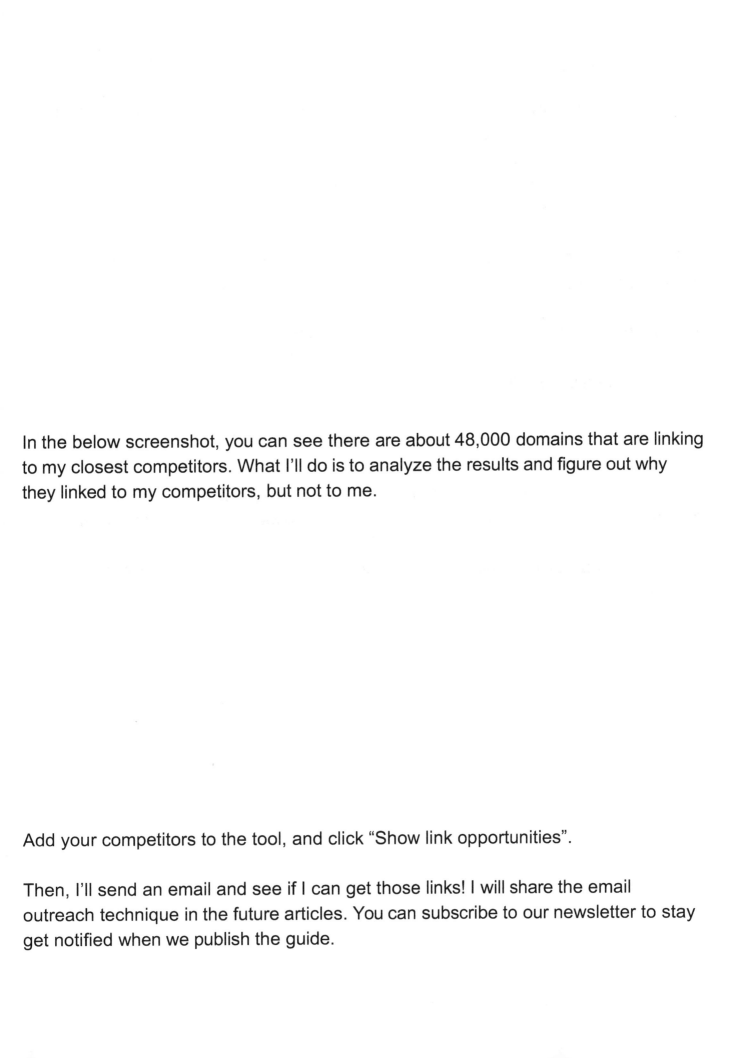

Add your competitors to the tool, and click "Show link opportunities".

Then, I'll send an email and see if I can get those links! I will share the email outreach technique in the future articles. You can subscribe to our newsletter to stay get notified when we publish the guide.

4. Broken link building

The Web is constantly evolving. Pages change, move or get deleted all the time. Broken links are links to pages that no longer exist.

Nobody likes that. Webmasters and searchers hate broken links because they contribute to poor user experience.

But, they still exist because webmasters are busy. It takes a lot of effort to continuously rid your site of broken links.

This strategy takes advantage of that. The concept is simple:

- You find a broken link
- You recreate the dead content
- You reach out to people linking to that dead content and ask them to link to your recreated version.

The most important part of this strategy is finding the right "broken" content to recreate and pitch. To do this, you'll need a tool that allows you to analyze backlinks.

Enter the domain of an authoritative, competing site into Ahrefs' Site Explorer. Then, go to the Best by links report, and filter by "HTTP 404 not found".

As you can see, the 2nd page of this screenshot is dead, but previously had 113 dofollow backlinks linking to it. That's a great opportunity!

The Wayback Machine tells me it used to be a post about the differences among metaphors, similes, and analogies.

Now all you have to do is to recreate this content and tell all 113 people to link to you instead.

5. Submit to web directories

Submitting your blog to web directories is another easy way to get backlinks.

With that said, this method is not very popular these days because finding a legal web directory is not easy. You must especially avoid those web directories that ask you to create a backlink to their website to get your website into their directory.

Also important: If you are using any automatic direct submission tactics, *stop doing so right away*. Automatic website submissions will cause your blog to appear as spam, and it can cost you a lot in terms of your domain authority or even the complete removal of your blog from search engines.

I hope this article will help you understand the basics of *backlinks in SEO*, and why you should start working on getting backlinks for your blog.

Do you currently work on getting backlinks for your blog? Tell us about your experiences in the comments section below.

Here are a few hand-picked guides for you to read next:

- Best Backlink Checker tools
- Best Google position checker tools

What Are Backlinks?

Backlinks (also known as "inbound links", "incoming links" or "one way links") are links from one website to a page on another website. Google and other major search engines consider backlinks "votes" for a specific page. Pages with a high number of backlinks tend to have high organic search engine rankings.

Other Website

Contains a link to your website

Your Website

Has a backlink from other website

For example, here is a link from Forbes to my website.

 Michael Wood, Contributor

Forbes

If you have ever done any research on backlinks, chances are you are familiar with the name Brian Dean. He is the founder of Backlinko, a website that provides case studies and strategies on how to generate backlinks the right way. He is a recognised SEO expert and if you type in any keyword related to backlinks, you will see his website at the top of the search results.

Because that link points directly to a page on my website, it's a "backlink".

Why Are Backlinks Important?

Backlinks are basically votes from other websites. Each of these votes tells search engines: "This content is valuable, credible and useful".

So the more of these "votes" you have, the higher your site will rank in Google and other search engines.

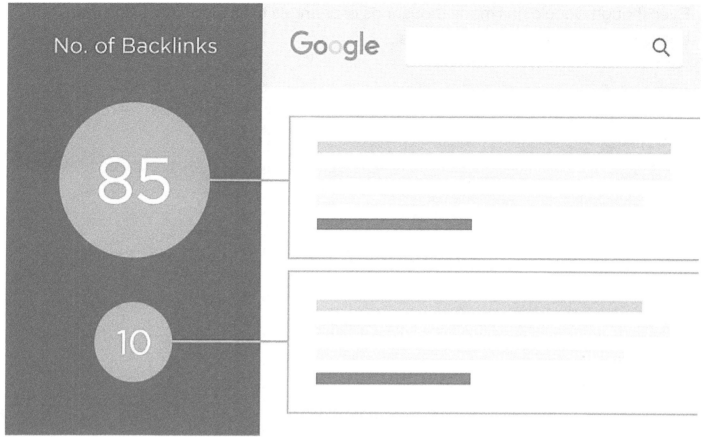

Using links in a search engine algorithm is nothing new. In fact, backlinks formed the foundation of Google's original algorithm (known as "PageRank").

The PageRank Citation Ranking:
Bringing Order to the Web

January 29, 1998

Abstract

The importance of a Web page is an inherently subjective matter, which depends on the readers interests, knowledge and attitudes. But there is still much that can be said objectively about the relative importance of Web pages. This paper describes PageRank, a method for rating Web pages objectively and mechanically, effectively measuring the human interest and attention devoted to them.

We compare PageRank to an idealized random Web surfer. We show how to efficiently compute PageRank for large numbers of pages. And, we show how to apply PageRank to search and to user navigation.

1 Introduction and Motivation

The World Wide Web creates many new challenges for information retrieval. It is very large and

Even though Google has made thousands of changes to its algorithm since then, backlinks remain a key ranking signal.

For example, an industry study that we conducted found that links remain Google's key ranking signal.

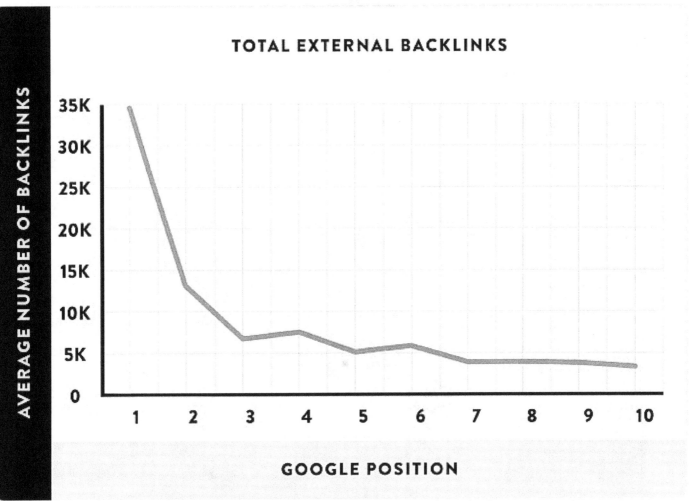

And Google has confirmed that backlinks remain one of their three most important search engine ranking factors.

Now we know: Here are Google's top 3 search ranking factors

Google's Andrey Lipattsev reveals links, content and RankBrain are the top three ranking signals in Google's search algorithm.

Barry Schwartz on March 24, 2016 at 7:32 am

What Types of Backlinks are Valuable?

Not all backlinks are created equal.

In other words, if you want to rank higher in the SERPs, focus on **quality** backlinks

backlinks. Put another way:

A single quality backlink can be more powerful than 1,000 low-quality

backlinks. As it turns out, high-quality backlinks tend to share the same key

traits.

Trait #1: They Come From Trusted, Authoritative Websites

Would you rather get a backlink from Harvard… or a random guy's website?

As it turns out, Google feels the same way.

This concept is known as "Domain Authority". Essentially, the more authority a site has, the more authority it can pass on to your site (via a link).

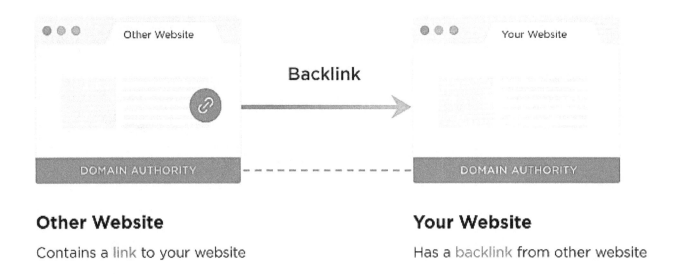

Other Website

Contains a link to your website

Your Website

Has a backlink from other website

For example, here's a link that I got from TechCrunch.

Backlinks, content and page speed are key

Backlinko recently teamed up with a handful of SEO software companies to evaluate the factors that are most important for success with SEO today. To do this, they analyzed one million Google search results.

Of the 20 potential ranking factors they looked at, five were revealed to be especially important. I'm going to deep-dive into these five important ranking factors, and show you how you can apply them to squeeze more juice out of your SEO efforts.

According to Ahrefs, TechCrunch is an extremely authoritative domain.

Because that link comes from an authority site, Google puts lots of weight on it. In fact, I noticed a boost in my organic search engine traffic right after TechCrunch linked to me.

Are these links hard to get?

Definitely. Are they worth it?

Absolutely.

Trait #2: They Include Your Target Keyword In The Link's Anchor Text
As a reminder, anchor text is the visible text part of a link.

ANCHOR LINKS

Anchor link on a webpage   Anchor link in code

In general, you want your links to have anchor text that includes your target keyword.

In fact, a recent industry study found a correlation between keyword-rich anchor text and higher rankings for that keyword.

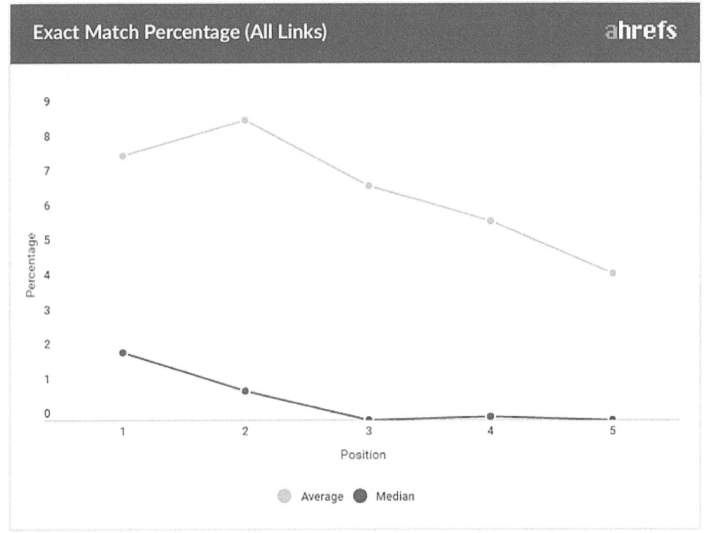

Now, a quick word of warning:

You don't want to go overboard with keyword-rich anchor text. In fact, Google has a filter in their algorithm called "Google Penguin".

Google Penguin filters out websites that use black hat link building strategies. And it specifically focuses on sites that build backlinks with exact match anchor text.

Trait #3: The Site (and Page) Linking to You Is Topically Related To Your Site

When a website links to another website, Google wants to see that the two sites are related.

This makes sense if you think about it:

Imagine you just published an article about running a marathon.

In that case, Google will put MUCH more weight on links from sites about marathons, running, fitness vs. sites about fishing, unicycles, and digital marketing.

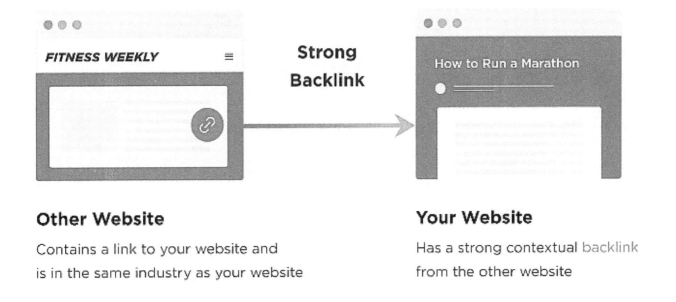

Other Website

Contains a link to your website and
is in the same industry as your website

Your Website

Has a strong contextual backlink
from the other website

Trait #4: The Link Is a "Dofollow" Link

Google and other search engines ignore links with the "nofollow" tag attached to it.

NOFOLLOW LINKS

```
<a href="https://yourwebsite.com" rel="nofollow">click here</a>
```

(In other words, nofollow links don't count search engine ranking algorithms).

Fortunately, the vast majority of links on the web are "dofollow" links.

And most of the links that have the nofollow tag aren't that valuable to begin with. For
example, links from these sources tend to be nofollow:

- Blog comments
- Press releases
- Paid advertisements

These links aren't super helpful for SEO anyway, so it's not a big deal that
they're nofollow.

Trait #5: The Link Is From a Domain That Hasn't Linked to You Before

Let's say you get a link from Website A.

Great.

Well, let's say Website A links to you again. And again. And

again. Are the 2nd, 3rd and 4th links as powerful as the first

one?

No.

As it turns out, links from the same website have diminishing returns.

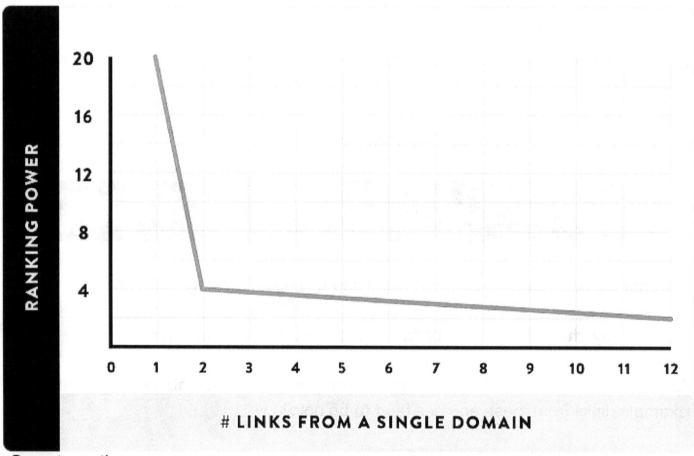

Or put another way:

It's usually better to get 100 links from 100 different websites than 1,000 links from the same website.

In fact, our search engine ranking correlation study found that the number of sites linking to you (not the total number of backlinks) correlated with Google rankings more than any other factor.

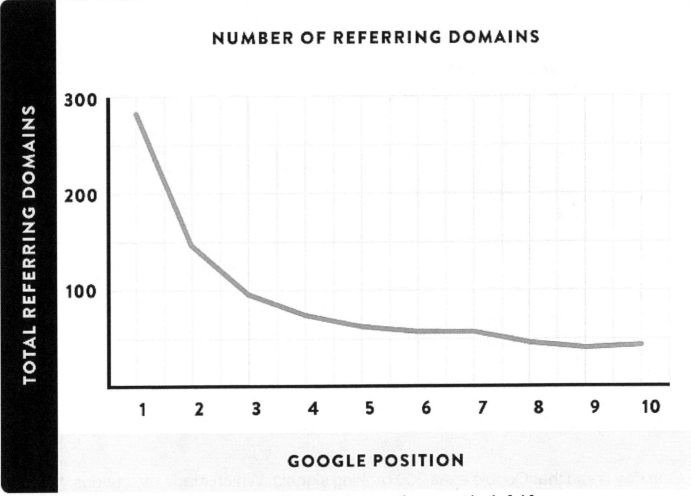

Now that you've seen what types of backlinks are the most helpful for your Google rankings, it's time for me to show you how to start building them.

Best Practices

Create a Linkable Assets

If you want people to link to your website, you need something on your site worth linking to.

(Also known as "Linkable Assets").

A Linkable Asset can be a blog post, a video, a piece of software, a quiz, a survey... basically anything that people will want to link to.

In most cases, your linkable asset will be an amazing piece of content (which is why search engine optimization and content marketing are so closely tied together).

For example, when I first started my blog, I published this list of 200+ Google ranking factors.

One day I read that Google uses 200 ranking signals. Which made me curious: "What are these 200 signals?".

Of course, Google wasn't about to announce them to the world. So I started compiling statements from Google and patents that I found online.

Compiling these 200 factors was extremely time-consuming (it took me over 2 weeks). But in the end, I FINALLY compiled a list of 200 ranking factors that Google might use in their algorithm.

To date, this single piece of content has generated over 25,000 backlinks from 4,450 domains.

Google's 200 Ranking Factors: The Complete List (201

backlinko.com/google-ranking-f

Ahrefs Rank	U
2,828	8

Backlinks	Referring domains
25.4K −7K	4.45K
Recent 37.9K	Recent 4.91K
Historical 92.5K	Historical 7.97K

How about another example?

One of my most successful posts to date (in terms of backlinks and organic traffic) is my ultimate guide to YouTube SEO.

YouTube SEO: How to Rank YouTube Videos in 2019

 by Brian Dean ⓘ Last updated Jan. 04, 2019

In this post I'm going to show you EXACTLY how to rank your YouTube videos.

In fact, this is the exact process that I used to grow my channel to **188,300 views per month.**

Last 28 days

Watch time (min)
931.1K
↑ 8%

Views
188.3K
↑ 7%

When I started writing this post I was starting to have some success with YouTube marketing. So I decided to compile and share what I learned in the form of an ultimate guide.

I also decided to include a lot of examples in my guide:

Step #1: YouTube Keyword Research

The YouTube SEO process begins with video keyword research.

Here's exactly how to find the right keywords for your YouTube videos:

First, generate a list of keywords ideas.

Your first step is to generate a big ol' list of potential keywords. Then, in the next step, I'll help you find the best keyword from your list.

Here's how to find keywords for your YouTube Videos:

One of my favorite strategies is to use the YouTube's Search Suggest feature.

Step #2: Publish a High-Retention Video

Here's the truth:

If you want your videos to rank, **you need to keep people watching.**

The amount of your video that people watch is known as Audience Retention.

And YouTube has gone on the record saying: "Audience Retention" is a HUGE ranking factor. To quote YouTube:

Step #3: YouTube Video Optimization

Here's how to extract the most SEO value from your video:

SAY Your Target Keyword

You've probably noticed that YouTube now automatically transcribes your videos. And at least in my experience, they're pretty darn accurate:

How to Get Higher Google Rankings in 2018 [New Checklist]

Step #4: Promote Your Video

We talked a lot about creating videos that maximize Audience Retention and user experience signals. Which is important.

But for YouTube to measure these signals, **you need to get views on your video!**

Here are some strategies you can use to get targeted views to your video:

Mention Your Video on Quora and Other Q&A Sites

Quora, forums and other Q&A sites are some of the most popular sites on the web for

(Something that most of the other content on this topic lacked)

Even though this post hasn't generated nearly the same amount of links as my Google Ranking Factors post, it's still racked up quite a few backlinks.

YouTube SEO: How to Rank YouTube Videos in 201

backlinko.com/how-to-ra

Ahrefs Rank [i]		Backlinks [i]	Referring domains [i]
2,828	5	2.55K +34	889
		Recent 3.12K	Recent 999
		Historical 27.8K	Historical 1.81K

Build Backlinks from Link Roundups

Imagine if people published blog posts with the sole purpose of linking out to quality content.

(The type of quality content that you publish on your site

already) It'd be pretty great, right?

Fortunately, that's a real thing. And they're called link

roundups. Here's an example:

Monthly Round Up: 10 Things that Happened in Digital Marketing in February

It's that special time of the month, Ricemedia's Monthly Roundup of the 10 biggest stories in SEO, PPC, Social Media and all things Digital Marketing. Even though February may be the shortest month of the year, don't expect it to be a quiet month.

Google To Shut Down Google Compare Products in US and UK On March 23

Yes, it is true. As of March 23rd, Google Compare will no longer be available to US and UK users. Whether the service will be relaunched as a different programme or be replaced by new service altogether, it is uncertain. For more, Search Engine Land's ha the latest. Read more

Facebook Reactions: Meet Facebook's New Supercharged 'Like' Button

It seems Facebook is all a buzz about their new reaction buttons and there's plenty of reasons why. A great blog covering this news is Buffer's own social media blog and they have a fantastic breakdown of these new buttons as well as what it could mean for social media marketing. Read more

Link roundups are daily, weekly or monthly blog posts that link to outstanding content.

Here's an example of a backlink that I recently built from a roundup:

HOME   ABOUT   CONTACT US   CONTENT MARKETING SERVICES   BLOG   ONLINE SE

The editorial team at Brafton posts "Marketers are killing their SEO content with bad headlines."

Brian Dean shares a brief post and infographic, "On-Page SEO: Anatomy of a Perfectly Optimized Page" at Backlinko.

Phil Nottingham discusses "How to Leverage Investment in Video to Build More Links" at The Moz Blog.

Here's the step-by-step process.

Find Link Roundups In Your Niche: Use search strings in Google search, like ""Keyword" + "link roundup".

Pitch Your Resource: (Gently) suggest that they include your linkable asset to the roundup.

And if your post is a good fit for that person's roundup, you'll get a high-quality link.

 Paul   Feb 7
to me

Hi Brian,

Thanks for contacting me. It took me around 0.000527 seconds to decide if your post was a good fit. I've just completed my roundup, you can find it here:

Love Backlinko by the way, great name great site.

Have a good weekend,

Regards,

Paul

(They may also share your content on social media)

Use The Moving Man

Method Here is the 3-step

process:

1. First, you find web pages, resources or businesses that are outdated, rebranded or recently changed names.
2. Then, find the sites that are still linking to these outdated resources.
3. Finally, you email people to let them know that they're linking to something that's out of date.

Let me show you how this works with a real-life example...

A while back I read that a website for a big SEO agency website suddenly shut down.

SEO Firm Made Of Giants, BlueGlass Is Collapsing

Apr 25, 2013 • 8:16 am | (26)
by Barry Schwartz | Filed Under SEM / SEO Companies

I have this policy of not covering topics here if (1) there are not communities talking about it in forum like settings and (2) if that community is not open, I won't talk about it. I only cover public threads and content that is available to anyone to see.

BlueGlass

Over the pass few weeks, I was invited into a private Facebook community talking about What Happened to BlueGlass - that is the title of the Facebook group. That group was set to "open" status a few days ago by former BlueGlass executive, Greg Boser.

To make a long story short, it seems like BlueGlass ran into some serious financial debt and cannot easily dig themselves out of it. Some history is that BlueGlass was formed by several well-known SEO companies and personalities in the industry. It was a merger of these "giant" names in the SEO community to form the ultimate SEO company.

This meant that they had lots of pages on their site that weren't working anymore...

…pages that lots of people were still linking to.

Specifically, I noticed that an infographic about SEO on their site wasn't working anymore. Which was perfect , because I had just published my own SEO-focused infographic.

So that was the first step.

Next, I had to see who actually linked to that

infographic. So I fired up Ahrefs and pulled all of their

Finally, I emailed everyone that linked to the infographic to let them know the image wasn't working anymore. I also let them know that my infographic would make a great replacement for the BlueGlass one.

Here's the script I used:

Hi [Name],

I was searching for some content to read about [Topic] this morning. And I came across your excellent post: [Post Title].

Anyway, I couldn't help but notice that you mentioned [Outdated Resource] in your article.

As you may have heard, [Problem With Outdated Resource].

Here's a screenshot of where that link is located: [Screenshot]

Also, I recently published a piece of content about [Topic]. It might make a good replacement for the [Outdated Resource].

Either way, I hope this helps you and have a great day!

Thanks,
[Your Name]

As you can see, people were more than happy to link to me:

to me ▾

Thanks Brian. That post is rather old and I haven't updated it for a while.
Obviously Google Reader no longer exists either. Anyway, I have removed Blueglass and added your link under the SEO/SEM category.

Broken Link Building

This strategy is similar to the Moving Man Method you just learned about.

The difference is that with broken link building, you're only looking for pages that have 404 errors.

To find these 404 links, you want to focus on resource pages in your niche. So if you're in the fitness niche you'd search in Google using these search strings:

- "fitness" + "resource page"
- "fitness" + "resources"
- "fitness" + "recommended
- sites" "fitness" + "links"

And you'd find pages like this.

WALKING AND FITNESS LINKS

There are many links within the pages of this walking site. Here are some additional links that you might find helpful.

Misc. Articles and fitness tips from the Walking Site

atozfitness.com - atozfitness contains more than 900 verified links to fitness & bodybuilding sites, with new training and nutrition articles updated weekly.

Active - Information on walking and other fitness activities. Event calendar. (Formerly Racegate.com)

American Volkssport Association - Looking for fun walks. This group host free walks all over the states. Look here for links to your state or the international organization.

Brazos Walking Sticks - We offer a wide variety of walking sticks and canes that you can use for a lifetime of walking and hiking enjoyment.

Now you could email the site owner and ask for a link. But I've found that begging doesn't work very well.

Instead, let the site owner know about any broken links that you find.

You can easily find broken links on any page. Just use the nifty Check My Links Chrome Extension.

This program quickly finds any broken links the page happens to have. It also highlights them in red to make them easy to find:

Newsfire - RSS reader for OS X

NetNewsWire - Newsgator's RSS reader for the Mac comes in two flavors: commercial and free

PixelNews - a commercial Mac OS X RSS reader that comes with a huge database of feeds

Shrook - a Mac RSS reader which also has a web based version; supports synchronization, instant notifications via Growl, real time search, smart grouping and more

Vienna 404 - a freeware, open source RSS/Atom newsreader, with a built-in tabbed browser and the ability to customize feed display

NewsLife - RSS reader for the Mac, pleasing to the eye, simple and easy to use

Squeet - another Mac RSS reader, currently on hiatus

The last thing you need to do is email the site owner about their dead

link. Hi [Site Owner Name],

I was just browsing around your resources page today, and among the lists of great resources, were some broken links.

Here's a few of them:

[URL 1]
[URL 2]
[URL 3]

Oh, and I have a website, [Your Website], that also regularly posts quality content related to whatever. If you think so too, feel free to post a link to it on your resources page.

Either way I hope this helps and keep up the good

work! Thanks,
[Your Name]

Guest Posting

Is guest posting

dead? Not really.

In fact, when you're first starting out, guest blogging is one of the BEST ways to get links to your site.

In fact, when I first started Backlinko, I wrote over 50 guest posts and interviews in 12 months!

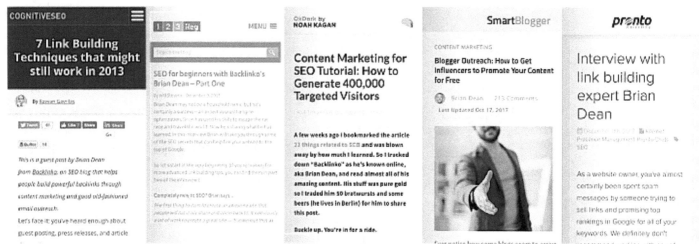

And the links I got from guest posting definitely gave my organic traffic a boost.

That said, I was very strategic about things. I made sure to only write guest posts for quality sites in my niche.

So if you run a site about the Paleo Diet, and write a guest post on a site about iPhones, that's going to look spammy to Google.

But when you write mind-blowing guest posts for quality websites in your industry, those links DO help.

The thing is, finding places to guest post can be a HUGE

pain. But there's an easier way…

Here's how it works:

First, find someone in your industry that writes a lot of guest posts.

Next, go to one of their published guest posts. And grab the headshot they use in their author bio:

Larry Kim In the Trenches

Larry Kim is the CEO of MobileMonkey, a chatbot building platform for marketers that enables mobile messaging between businesses and customers via Facebook Messenger. He's also the founder of WordStream, the World's top PPC marketing software company. You can subscribe to Kim's business growth tips by email, or connect on LinkedIn, Twitter and Facebook.

@larrykim

MARKETING
10 Places You Can Promote Your Business for Free

SOCIAL MEDIA TOOLKIT
10 Content Ideas to Make Your Social Media Stand Out

Let Elon Musk-Jack Ma Debate About the Future of AI. But Its Business Impact Is Already Here Today.

Finally, pop the URL of that screenshot into Google reverse image search.

And you'll get a list of places that published guest posts on.

Pages that include matching images

Who Is MobileMonkey? Meet the Team

https://mobilemonkRy.com › our-team •

 z4g • 349 - Larry Kim. GEO. Larry founded MDbileMonkey in 2D17 after seeing the need for a product that enables marketers to engage with customers via mobile ...

Larry Kim — Medium

https://medium.com › •

 256 256 - Read writing from Larry Kim on Medium. CEO of MobifeMonkey. Founder of WordStream. Top columnist @Inc AdWords, Facebook Advertising, Marketing, ..

MarTech Interview with Larry Kim, CEO at MobileMonkey

https://martechseries.com › mts-insights › interviews › martech-interview-I... •

 400 • 40D - 10 Oct 2D19 - The MarTech Interview Series with Larry Kim, CEO at MobileMonkey is a fun Q&A style chat. It follows a two part format On Marketing ...

AiThority Interview with Larry Kim, CEO at MobileMonkey

https://www.aithority.com › interviews › ait-megamind › aithority-intervie... •

 160D ^ 900 - ZS Oct 2019 - The AiThority Interview Series with Larry Kim, CEO at MobileMonkey is an AI-centric chat on AI/ML and Chatbots.

Why Facebook Messenger Banned My Page 8 What I'm Doing ...

https://mobilemonkey.com › Dlog › Facebook Messenger News & Policy •

 50 50 - Limits have been placed on Larry Xim ... When I created my chatbot sequence in MobileMonkey, I tried to make ft ... Check out Larry Kim as an actual unicorn.

Infographics and Other Visual Assets

Do infographics work as well as they used to? Probably

not. But they're still an effective link building strategy.

In fact, when we looked at what types of content generate the most links, infographics came out near the top.

"WHY POSTS", "WHAT POSTS" AND INFOGRAPHICS ARE HEAVILY LINKED TO

TYPE OF POST	REFERRING DOMAINS
WHY POST	3.2
WHAT POST	2.8
INFOGRAPHIC	2.7
VIDEO	2.5
GENERAL POST	2.4
HOW-TO POST	2.3
LIST POST	2.1

For example, one of the first infographics I ever made took only took a few hours to put together (I also hired a professional designer to make it look professional).

12 KEY ON-PAGE SEO FACTORS THAT SEARCH ENGINES (AND USERS) LOVE

Even though this infographic didn't go viral, it led to some solid backlinks:

On-Page SEO: Anatomy of a Perfectly Optimized Page (Infographic)

💬 9 COMMENTS   SEO

An infographic that shows you how to SEO your web pages

Struggling to know how to optimize your website for the search engines? Brian Dean of Backlinko has published a very pretty infographic showing just that.

To be clear: I didn't just publish my infographic and hope for the best.

Like any piece of content that you publish, you need to strategically promote your infographic. And to do that, I recommend using a strategy called "Guestographics".

I outline exactly how Guestographics work in this

post. Submit Testimonials

Companies big and small love to show off customer testimonials.

And you're using a product or service that you love (or at least like), consider sending them a testimonial.

To show that you're a real person they'll often add a link to your website… without you even having to ask.

Here's an example:

Convert Your Website Visitors Into Paying Customers: How One Couple Did It With Email Marketing

In July of 2014 alone, Shane and Jocelyn Sams made over $140,000. Let that sink in for a minute.

The couple isn't printing money or selling baby unicorns. They're simply online marketers who know a thing or two about connecting with an audience, something they teach on their website Flipped Lifestyle.

But they weren't always experts.

Blogger Reviews

If you have a piece of software, physical product, consulting service or ANYTHING of value that you sell, you can easily turn that into dozens of high-quality backlinks.

How?

By offering your product to bloggers for

free. Here's how:

HOW TO MAKE HOMEMADE SOAP IN A CROCKP T {A PH ›T‹- TUT ›RIAL)

This post has been a year and a half in the making. I hope you2l be as excited about it as I am! ;-)

1. Find bloggers in your niche that might be interested in what you have to offer. If you sell an information product that teaches people how to make their own soaps, you'd Google things like "soap making", "make soap at home" etc.
2. Your results will be a mixed bag of blogs, news websites and "how to" websites like eHow. Filter out how-to sites or news sites. You'll be left with a solid list bloggers that might be interested in your offer, like this one:
3. Reach out to them with this email script:

Hey [Site Owner Name],

I was searching for [Some Homemade Soap Recipes] today when I came across [Website].

Awesome stuff!

Actually, I just launched a guide that [Teaches People How To Make Luxury Soaps At Home]. I usually charge [$X], but I'd be more than happy to send it over to you on the house.

Let me know how that

sounds. Cheers,
[Your First Name]

One word of warning: You want to be VERY careful about the language you use for this strategy.

Note how you don't offer your product in exchange for a link or review… which would violate Google's Webmaster Guidelines.

Instead, send them the product and let them decide if it's worth a mention on their blog.

Link Reclamation

Link reclamation is simple:

First, find mentions of your company that don't link to your

site. Here's an example:

Content length: According to Backlinko, the average length of a first-page result on Google is 1,890 words. Length is a general indicator of quality, so fill your site with comprehensive, valuable content that users will read in full.

GMB page: The title and content of your GMB page must be relevant to local users.

Page title: Include your main keywords here

See how the author of that article above mentioned my website… but didn't link to

it? That's where link reclamation comes into play.

Instead of saying "I wish they linked to me", you proactively reach out and ask them to link.

In my experience, a friendly reminder is usually enough to get most people to log into WordPress and add your link.

Here's the step-by-step process:

Content Alerts for backlinko - mentions

Keyword: backlinko   Min 0 Shares

☑ Edit   ⟳ Refresh

Why You Should Start Advertising Your Google+ Posts

jaysonlinereviews.com

By Jayorban

…Website Or Blog"Hottest Most Powerful Backlink Sources For Marketers In 2014 To Improve Your Serp Positioning In The Search Engines"   1. **Backlinko** has…

	3	1	1	0	1
Total Shares: 6					

How to Ideate, Create, and Promote Valuable Content to Increase Everything - Ahrefs Blog

blog.ahrefs.com

By Andrew Herrault

…content topic before. Brian Dean from **Backlinko** describes how to do just that using Ahrefs (OpenSiteExplorer works too), a link scraper, in the third…

	1	1	5	1	1
Total Shares: 9					

1. Use a tool like BuzzSumo and Mention.com to find mentions of your brand online. **When you do, you'll get a heads up whenever someone writes about you:**

2. Check to see whether or not the person that mentioned you also linked back to your site (either your homepage or internal page). If they linked to your site, you're set.
   If not, move onto step #3...

3. Send them this friendly email.
   Hey [Name],

   I just wanted to reach out and say "thanks" for mentioning [Your Brand] in your excellent article yesterday.

   We really, really appreciate it.

   I'm reaching out today to ask if you could add a link back to our site. That way, people can easily find us while reading your article.

   Either way, thanks for the shout out and keep up the great work!

   Thanks,
   [Your First Name]

Use HARO

HARO (short for Help a Reporter Out) is one of the best ways to get high authority backlinks from news sites.

Here's how HARO works:

3) Summary: How companies are addressing project-related security risks

Category: High Tech

Email: query-7528@helpareporter.net

Media Outlet: Anonymous

Deadline: 7:00 PM PST - 21 August

Query:

Re: security related risks in projects/initiatives (mobile security risks with remote teams or anything relating to cyber-security risks).

1) What are the risks and concerns around project/team communications?

2) How do these security issues impact your projects/initiatives?

3) What is your business doing to overcome/address the issues? If using a solution provider, please mention factors behind vendor/solution selection and how the solution resolved any issues.

Back to Top Back to Category Index

1. Sign Up To HARO as a source here.
2. You'll get three emails per day from reporters looking for sources, like this one:
3. Respond with your credentials and some helpful tips.

Easy right? You give a reporter a quote and they'll hook you up with a backlink.

That's all there is to it.

For example, recently got a sweet link from Entrepreneur.com by replying to a HARO request:

5. Identifying dead businesses

While new businesses are created every day, a lot of existing businesses die.

Brian Dean, the founder of SEO training company, Backlinko says he regularly identifies websites in his industry that have shut shop. Analyzing their backlink profiles will help you identify a number of links from high authority websites that are linking to the now-dead website. Brian says he has been able to get a lot of these websites to replace their outdated links with new resources on his website by just emailing them.

Reverse Engineer Your Competitor's Backlinks

Every industry has its own set of link building opportunities.

So I recommend setting aside some time to reverse engineer your competition. That way, you can find link opportunities that only exist in your niche.

How about an example?

Let's say you run a health and fitness

blog. And one of your competitors is Nerd

Fitness.

Well, when I check out that site's link profile in a backlink checker, I notice that A LOT of their links come from podcasts:

Well, my guest on the podcast today argues that perhaps there's actually a thing or two we can learn from how video games are designed that can help improve our real life. His name is Steve Kamb and he's the owner of Nerd Fitness. In Steve's newly published book, *Level Up Your Life*, he shows readers how they can use the same mechanics that make video games so fun and addicting to help them get in better shape and knock off items on their bucket list.

Show Highlights

- How Steve stumbled upon the idea of using video game mechanics to improve his real life

Specifically, people from that company (especially the founder, Steve Kamb) appear on other people's podcasts as guests.

Just like that you have a nice list of places that you can go to get links.

(Obviously, you need to reach out to the people that run those podcasts and pitch yourself as a guest. Which takes work. But at least you know where to start).

Stick to Content Formats That Generate Links

Like I mentioned earlier, infographics are one content format that's ideal for building backlinks.

But it's one of many.

We also found that, even though they didn't generate lots of social media shares, "Why posts" and "What posts" tended to get linked-to fairly often.

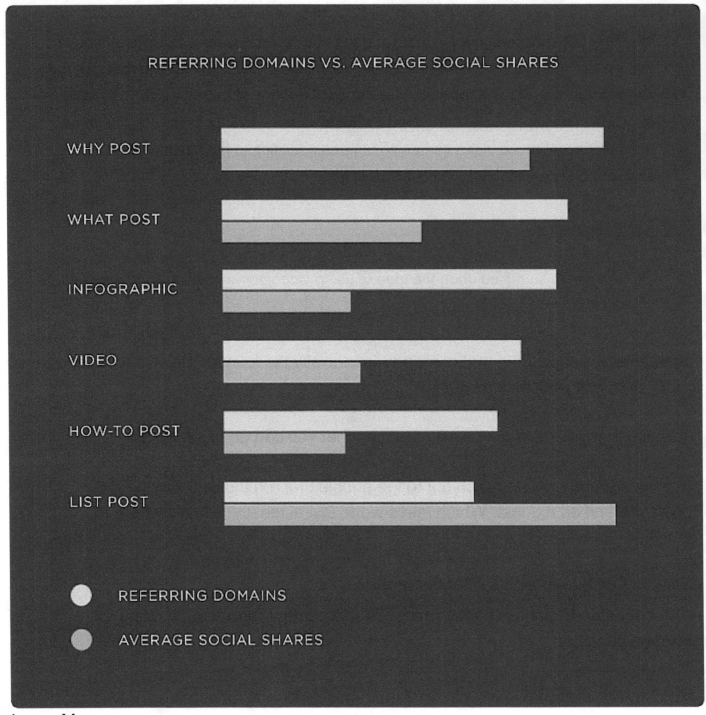

Learn More

Link Building: How to Get Powerful Backlinks: Video tutorial that shows you how to build backlinks to your site using white hat SEO techniques.

How to Get High Quality Backlinks (7 New Strategies): This is an updated list of link building strategies that focus on building new backlinks from authority websites.

15 Awesome Link Building Tools: If you're serious about link building, you'll need tools to

help you do the job. Here's a list of the best of the bunch.

How to Do a Basic Backlink Analysis on Your Competitors: Learn how to evaluate your competitors backlinks.

10 Smart Ways to Earn or Build Backlinks to Your Website

"Backlinks," meaning sites that link to your site, are, for most search engines, the supreme ranking factor. So is getting more organic traffic.

Because that traffic is directly related to the *quality* of the backlinks your website has, the more authoritative websites that link to you, the better rankings and traffic you'll get.

And of course you want to keep an eye on your Google rankings. When crawling the web, Google looks in particular for your website's backlinks, to understand how your pages are connected to one other and in what ways. Certainly there are hundreds of ranking factors. But backlinks represent the most important metric for SEO.

Now, needless to say, quality backlinks are hard to get, but they shouldn't be. In fact there are smart ways to build or earn backlinks, to get authoritative websites to link to your online business. Here are ten:

1. The broken-link building method

I love the broken-link building method because it works perfectly to create one-way backlinks. The technique involves contacting a webmaster to report broken links on his/her website. At the same time, you recommend other websites to replace that link. And here, of course, you mention your own website. Because you are doing the webmaster a favor by reporting the broken links, the chances of a backlink back to your website are high.

So, to use the broken-link method, first find relevant websites in your niche that have resources pages. Find them by using these search queries in Google:

- your keyword + links
- your keywords + resources
- keywords inurl:links

Now, back to that webmaster: When reaching out, be friendly and introduce yourself. Tell this individual that he or she is linking to some resources that are no longer available. Always provide the exact location of the broken links, so they can be easily found. Give some alternatives to replace those links, including your own website. Try to be helpful, not greedy to get a backlink. Often, this method will work, but there will be cases when the webmaster will refuse to link back to you.

2. Backlinks through infographics

Infographics are one of the most popular methods for bringing traffic to your website and gaining valuable backlinks. They're also great because they're easy to understand and share. Everyone loves visual data, right? That's why the demand for infographics has increased considerably. Consider that influential online publications like Mashable publish numerous infographics from all over the Internet.

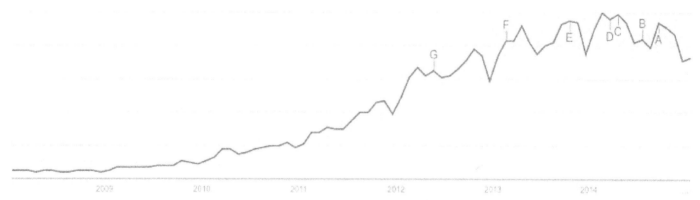

Now, choose your infographics carefully: Each one should include a unique and interesting story for your audience. To make your selection, follow currently trending topics and see what people are looking for, then create your infographic using statistical data.

To get started, research and gather data for the content. Then find someone to make your content visual.

There's a misconception that creating an infographic is expensive; that's not always the case. Figure on an average price between $150 and $300. Assuming you may earn 10 backlinks per infographic, you'll be paying $15 per link. For five backlinks, the price will be $30 per link. That's very cheap for backlinks earned through webmaster moderation. And if your infographic goes viral. you win even more.

Try using Dribble to find designers with good portfolios. Contact them directly by upgrading your account to PRO status, for just $20 a year. Then simply use the search filter and type "infographics." After finding someone you like, click on "hire me" and send a message detailing your needs and requesting a price. Fiver is another place to find great designers willing to create inexpensive infographics.

Next, once the infographic is ready, you need to make it easy for others to share it. To do this, create your own embed code using Siege Media generator.

SETTINGS

Site Name:	YourDomain.com	Embed Box Width:	540px
Post URL:	http://domain.com/post-url/	Embed Box Height:	100px
Image URL:	http://domain.com/image.jpg		
Image Alt:	Infographic Name		
Width of Image:	540px		
Height of Image:	Leave empty to keep proportion.		

USE THIS CODE

```
<h3>Share this Image On Your Site</h3><textarea
onclick='this.focus();this.select{}'
style='width:540px;height:100px'><p>
<strong>Please include attribution to site name
goes here Here with this graphic.</strong><br />
<br /><a href=''><img src='' alt='' width=''
border='0'/></a></p></textarea>
```

RESULTS PREVIEW

SHARE THIS IMAGE ON YOUR SITE

```
<p><strong>Please include attribution to site name goes here
Here with this graphic.</strong><br /><br /><a href=''><img
src='' alt='' width='' border='0'/></a></p>
```

Once everything is in place, and your infographic shines on your website, it's time to distribute it. There are numerous infographic directories where you can submit yours. For example, here is a list with more than than 100 places to submit your infographic.

Last but not least, do email outreach to people who have previously linked to similar infographics or have shared them on social media. Ask for feedback on your infographic, but never ask for a link directly. If they like your infographic, they'll know what to do.

3. The advantage of guest articles

Guest blogging is the most effective way to reach new audiences. By publishing articles on other popular websites, you'll get your content in front of new readers and win more exposure. Sometimes, it's not just about the backlink, but about increasing your online reputation or your social media followers.

Guest blogging helps you leverage your relationships and expand your audience. In case you have doubts about guest posting, consider that even Google accepts guest contributors on its Google Analytics blog. Here's a tweet from Google showing this:

Numerous ways exist to find websites that accept guest articles. Here are three::

Use Google search queries to find blogs accepting guest contributors:

- your keyword + inurl:write-for-
- us your keyword + guest-posts
- your keyword + inurl:guest-post-guidelines
- your keyword + become a contributor
- your keyword + bloggers
- wanted your keyword + submit
- an article your keyword + want
- to write for your keyword + contribute
- your keyword + become an
- author your keyword + guest post by
- your keyword + now accepting guest posts

Find influencers publishing guest posts on a regular basis and try to contribute on the same websites they've had in the past.

Consider the example of a profile by freelance writer Kristi Hines. From her Google Plus profile, click on "About," then scroll to the contributor section, where you can see a list of all the websites she has contributed articles to.

Contributor to

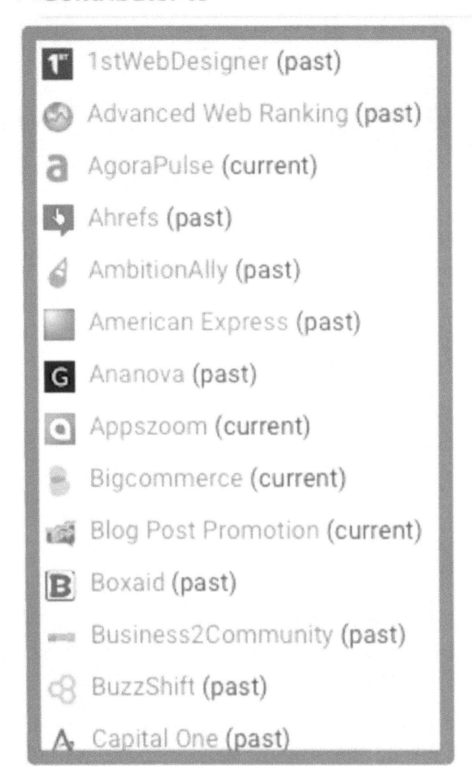

- 1stWebDesigner (past)
- Advanced Web Ranking (past)
- AgoraPulse (current)
- Ahrefs (past)
- AmbitionAlly (past)
- American Express (past)
- Ananova (past)
- Appszoom (current)
- Bigcommerce (current)
- Blog Post Promotion (current)
- Boxaid (past)
- Business2Community (past)
- BuzzShift (past)
- Capital One (past)

Repeat the process with other influencers, and you'll find endless opportunities to publish content on third-party websites.

Use social media to discover other options.

On Twitter, search for "guest post," "guest article" or "guest author." To automate the process, use Topsy to set alerts for the keywords you want to track.

When publishing a guest article, always make sure you are linking to your social media profiles. If someone enjoys your post, he or she can easily follow you for similar future articles.

4. Spy on your competitors.

If you are serious about getting more organic traffic, staying up to date with your main competitors' online marketing strategies is mandatory. You have to spy on your competitors on social media and look for their link-building or earning techniques, as well as their content-marketing methods. Here are some tips:

Set yourself up for alerts when competitors are publishing new content on their websites.

Subscribe to their email newsletters or follow them on social media. Another smart way to catch up with their new content is to create a Google alert for the keyword "site:yourcompetitor.com." For example, if my competitor is TechCrunch, I can set a Google alert using the keyword: site:techcrunch.com

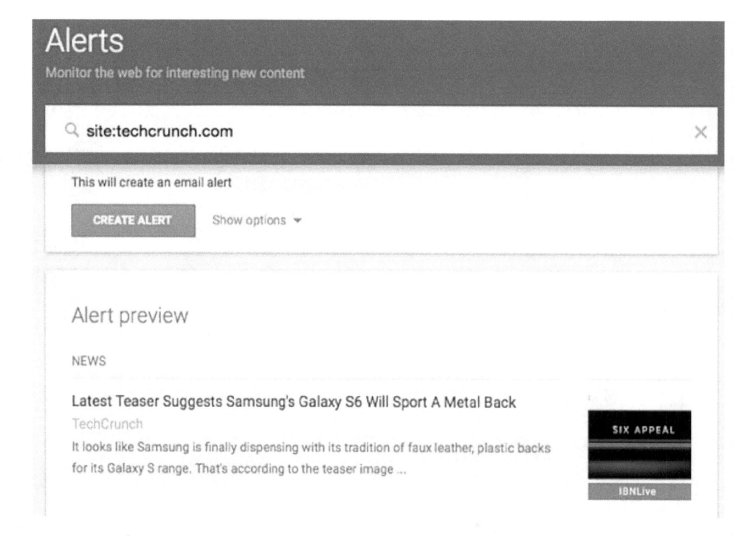

Know when and what backlinks your competitors are building or earning.

This will help you replicate their best backlinks and better understand what methods they are using to promote their website. If they are getting links through guest blogging, try to become a guest author on the same websites. If most of their links come from blog reviews, get in touch with those bloggers and offer them a trial to test your tool.

Eventually, they might write a review about it.

My favorite tool to spy on my competitors' backlinks is called Monitor Backlinks. It allows you to add your four most important competitors. From then on, you get a weekly report containing all the new links they have earned. Inside the tool, you get more insights about these links and can sort them by their value and other SEO metrics. A useful feature is that all the links my own website already has are highlighted in green, as in the screenshot below.

Links to matthewwoodward.co.uk

#	📅	Ahrefs Page	Ahrefs Domain	Status	URL From	URL To	Anchor	External Links	TLD	IP
	Feb 15, 2015										
1	Feb 04	32	45	NOFOLLOW	kekefireworks.com	/income-reports/	18+	1904		
2	Feb 06	26	53	OK	yourdreamblog.c...	/experiments/h...	Banner Ads	54		

Using this technique, I can easily determine new link-building opportunities. With Monitor Backlinks, I can keep track of all the backlinks my website is earning. Each time my link building campaigns are successful, I can see all the new backlinks I'm getting in my dashboard.

5. Build internal links.

Internal links are a key factor for running a successful blog. They are passing link juice, and you can use your anchor texts. With a good internal linking structure, you can help users easily navigate through your website and increase the overall user experience.

There are tools that can automatically create internal links on your blog, especially if you are running Wordpress, but you should do this manually. Microsoft's Matt Cutts has recommended that webmasters keep their number of internal links per page below 100, for both usability and SEO.

6. Promote your content.

Great content won't get you backlinks unless you know how to promote it right. You have to get out in the world and do email outreach to promote your best articles.

One of the best strategies to do this is to contact bloggers or websites running weekly or monthly roundups. Again, you can use Google and search for queries like "keyword + roundup." Make sure you choose, in order to see results only from the past week or month.

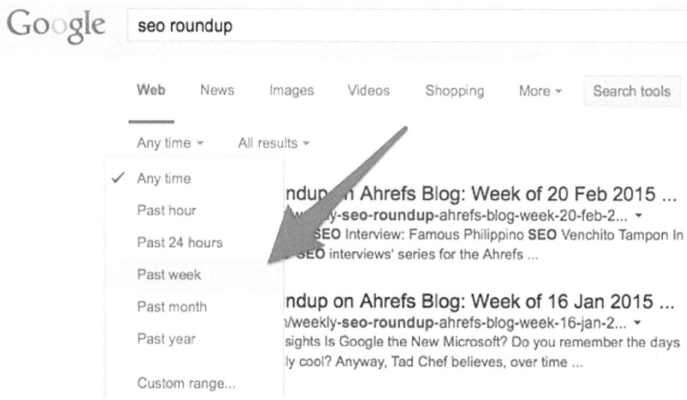

Then contact the webmasters and give them a quick introduction to your website. With your message, send a link to one of your best tutorials or guides. If they find your resource useful, they may link back to you in their next weekly roundup.These bloggers are constantly looking for great content, so they definitely want to hear from you.

As with the other techniques, make sure you do not abuse your relationship with any webmaster by asking for a link directly.

7. Write testimonials.

An easy method to earn quality backlinks is to write testimonials for websites you are using. You'll spend only a few minutes, and you can earn a link from the homepage of an authoritative website. As long as you are a customer of that product, there's a high possibility you can get a link in exchange for a testimonial.

We now have 15 major keywords in top 3 positions. We've had a record start to the year due to a large boost in leads.

Ben Cooper
Club Coops

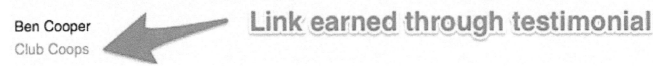 Link earned through testimonial

List all the tools you are currently using and reach out to discuss the likelihood of featuring your testimonial on a desired website.

8. Contact journalists and important bloggers.

To get links to your website, you have to spread the word about your business. And what better way to do this than email outreach to journalists and influencers from your niche? Fnding someone's email address can be challenging, but there's no reason to be discouraged. Here's how to find anyone's email address:

SUCCESS

Yes! I've found them!

felix@prooptimization.com

Search another   My rates

Earning quality backlinks can sometimes be challenging, but you can easily find link-building opportunities by using the right resources and methods. Finally, remember that keeping your backlinks is as important as building them. So, keep track of the backlinks your website is getting, by using tools like Monitor Backlinks, Ahrefs or Majestic.

- Over 90 percent of the email addresses at publications and websites are formatted like this: john@website.com or sjohn@website.com or smith.john@website.com. So, try sending your pitch to these emails directly.
- **If the above formats don't work, use tools like Voilanorbert, Thrust.io or Emailfinder.io. Just enter the name of the person you are trying to contact and the website he or she works for.**

- **Alternately, you can send your message using social media, with Google Plus or Linkedin.**

Also consider that every pitch should be short and to the point. No one has time for long and boring emails from strangers.

9. Donate.

Yes, you can earn backlinks by donating to nonprofit organizations. This method is quick and straightforward. All you have to do is find websites in your niche that accept donations and link back to sites that have donated. Simply submit the amount of the donation you want to make and write your website URL.

Finding these websites requires some searches in Google. These are some queries that usually give good results:

- contributors page + donate + your
- keyword donation + contributors + your
- keyword contributors page + your keyword

10. Get interviewed.

Online interviews are hot right now, and a great and easy way to earn backlinks to your website. Once you become the authority in your niche, you'll get lots of interview invitations, but until then, to get started, you have to make the first step. Look for websites that are running interviews and tell them you would like to participate and what knowledge you can contribute.

Conclusion

How to Build Backlinks in 2020 (NEW Guide)

Backlinks are the nitrous of every successful SEO campaign.

This new guide will teach how to build backlinks in 2020. Every strategy you will read is battle tested.

Through hundreds of successful SEO campaigns, we now know what does and does NOT work.

Ready to get started? Start watching (or reading):

Want to become a link building expert in 2020? We dedicate all of Module 4 inside Gotch SEO Academy to it. Join over 750 other link building experts today.

What are Backlinks (and How Do They Work)?

A "backlink" is created when an external website links to yours. This why some people refer to them as "external backlinks" or "inbound links".

Here's how it looks in action:

These links are a large piece of the ranking puzzle.

But before we get into the heavy link building strategy…

You need to make sure that your site is <u>ready</u> for backlinks.

When to Build Backlinks

Many people dive into link acquisition before they've built a strong foundation. What you must realize is that a strong foundation (a well-optimized website) makes your link building more effective.

When your backlinks are more effective, you don't need as many to achieve your desired result!

That ultimately saves you time and money.

So, here's what you need to cover before jumping into link building:

1. Fix All Technical/UX Issues

Technical issues can hurt User Experience (UX) and UX is correlated to SEO performance (or lack of it).

View this as a foundational stage of the process.

That's because if speed through this process, you backlinks won't be as

effective. And what happens when your backlinks aren't as effective?

You have to acquire more, which costs your company more

money. Here are some technical/UX issues you need to look for:

- Site loading speed (use Google's PageSpeed
- Insights) Mobile friendliness (use Google's Mobile
- Friendly check) Duplicate content (use Siteliner)
- Canonical errors
- Duplicate META data
- Incorrect uses of directives (noindex, nofollow,

etc) Redirect Chains

Sometimes the most obvious solutions are right in front of your face. Redirect chains are another simple problem that can boost your site's authority once fixed.

This is what a redirect chain looks like:

Do you see the problem with this picture?

The problem is that "Page B" is acting as a buffer between "Page A" and the final destination "Page C".

This technical issue is robbing "Page C" of authority.

To fix this you need to 301 redirect "Page A" to "Page C" like so:

By fixing a redirect chain you will send authority/link equity directly to the

page. That is more effective than making the link equity pass through a

buffer.

302s

There's some debate on whether or not PageRank passes through 302 redirects. For many years, SEOs (including myself) have always stated that you should change 302s to 301s. This is still my stance. However, he's what Gary Illyes said about the topic: "30x redirects don't lose PageRank anymore."

Is Gary telling the truth? Probably.

But I still don't think it's worth the risk.

Out of the hundreds of SEO audits I've conducted, I've seen a few websites using 302s for their actual purpose (a temporary redirect).

In most cases 302s are nothing more than

accidental. With that said:

It's my preference to change 302s to 301s if they aren't being used for their actual purpose.

Reclaim Lost Link Juice (404 Link Reclamation)

404 link reclamation is at the top of the list because it is the easiest.

You can use Google Search Console to find 404s (Crawl > Crawl Errors > Not Found):

You can also use Screaming Frog to find 404 as well (Response Codes > Client Error – 4xx):

Then to see what 404 error pages have backlinks, just use Ahrefs' or Majestic's bulk analysis tools.

I recommend doing both just in case you miss some links.

When you find pages with link equity, you must 301 redirect them to a relevant page on the site or to your homepage.

Fix Broken External Links

Every external link you place on your site leaks authority.

That's why it's important to audit your site (here's an SEO audit checklist) to find broken external links.

This applies to both external links in your content and in the comment section.

You can easily find these broken external links using Ahrefs.

Go to "Outgoing links" and click "Broken Links".

You can use Screaming Frog SEO Spider to find most of these issues such 302 redirects, redirect chains, 404 errors, canonical errors, duplicate META data and incorrect uses of directives.

2. Develop a Strong Site Architecture

Developing an intelligent site architecture is the single best way to get the most "bang for your buck" when it comes to link building.

My favorite site architecture strategy is to use a reverse silo.

Instead of trying to acquire backlinks to non-linkable pages (homepages, category pages, product pages, etc), the reverse silo is built to acquire backlinks to content-rich pages.

These may be blog posts or individual information-driven pages.

Here's how it works:

This is a more effective approach for link acquisition because people are much more willing to link to valuable information than sales-driven pages.

With that said:

The ultimate goal of the reverse silo is to distribute link authority (PageRank) from your content assets to your sales-driven pages (via internal linking).

I believe this content-centric approach is the safest way to grow your site's authority.

Bringing me to the next point:

3. Create Linkable Assets

Every effective link building campaign should begin with creating linkable assets.

First, what is a linkable asset?

A linkable asset is usually a blog post or page that is informationally-driven.

For example, this blog post you're currently reading is a linkable asset. It's designed to educate and add value to my industry.

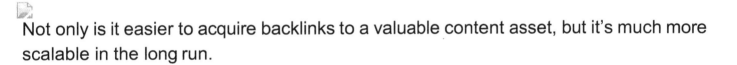

Not only is it easier to acquire backlinks to a valuable content asset, but it's much more scalable in the long run.

That's because you can continue to earn new backlinks overtime without much additional effort. That is, if you created the content the right way.

Read my guide on how to create SEO content to learn more.

At this stage, your website is on a strong foundation so it's time to start building backlinks, right?

Wait a second.

You need to have a clear understanding of what a "quality" link opportunity looks like before you dive in.

This will help:

7 Backlink Quality Indicators

Not all backlinks are created equally and that's why it's critical that you know what a good backlink look like. Here are some guidelines to follow:

1. Relevance

Your #1 link building objective should be to get backlinks on websites that are relevant to yours.

But don't take my word for it. Here's what a former member of Google's search quality team, Andre Weyher, said back in 2012:

> Not only this but take PR for example, getting a link from a high PR page used to always be valuable, today it's more the relevance of the site's theme in regards to yours, relevance is the new PR. – Andre Weyher

This quote is stating the obvious:

Your link acquisition efforts should begin with the most relevant opportunities.

But there's a problem with this approach:

Getting 100% exact relevancy for every single link is unrealistic.

That's why I develop The Relevancy Pyramid framework for prioritizing your link opportunities.

The Relevancy Pyramid

Here's a visual

representation:

The idea is quite simple.

There is a limited supply of 100% relevant link opportunities. However, as you broaden your research, there will be many more opportunities to go after.

The key is prioritize opportunities at the top of the pyramid (since they're the most relevant) and work your way down the pyramid (towards less relevant opportunities).

Let me show you how it would work with a more practical example.

I'm going to show you how I would prioritize opportunities for a supplement company.

Tier One: 100% Relevancy

I will designate a "1" to any opportunities that are 100% relevant to the supplement company. An example of 100% relevancy would be a website that reviews supplements. Or, a website that focuses on a specific supplement that the client offers like creatine.

As you can imagine, 100% relevant opportunities are few and far between. This is especially true in the "supplement" industry. That's because supplement companies create micro supplement sites to persuade you. So the chances of landing a link are low.

Tier Two: 75% Relevancy

All opportunities that are 75% relevant get a "2" designation. On this tier you would want to focus on "body building" opportunities.

Tier Three: 50% Relevancy

On tier three, you would focus on all "fitness" opportunities and assign a "3" to them.

The fitness space has unlimited opportunities.

First, you would focus on pure "fitness" blogs. After that, you could move onto any type of sports, CrossFit, or runner blogs.

It would likely take a year to tap into all the opportunities within this relevancy tier.

Tier Four: 25% Relevancy

On tier four, you would focus on "health" opportunities and assign a "4" to them.

There are countless websites about "health" in general. But, you can also tap into nutrition, elderly health, women's health, and men's health blogs.

Tier Five: 0% Relevancy

On tier five, you would focus on more "general" opportunities.

For example, if I link to the fall outfits guide on Joyfully Styled, it won't be as effective a "Tier 1" opportunity. That's because SEO and fashion aren't relevant to each other.

But, that doesn't mean the link I injected won't work.

We classify "general" (Tier 5) opportunities as authoritative news sites, colleges, and unrelated, but high-quality blogs.

You would assign a "5" to these opportunities.

News sites such as Huffington Post, Fox, CNN, or Yahoo would be targets on this tier.

You are likely wondering what "unrelated, but high-quality blogs" are…

Let me explain.

You would want to ask yourself:

Does the supplement company have a CEO who would like to share success secrets?

If the answer is "Yes", then focus on entrepreneur, business, small business, sales, marketing, and Internet marketing blogs.

You would also want to consider productivity or self improvement blogs. That's because both topics could incorporate supplements in one way or another.

Now that you understand the Relevancy Pyramid model, here's how it would actually look in practice:

I wouldn't normally color code, but I wanted you to see the different tiers.

The cool thing about this process is that you can outsource the entire

thing.

So, what I just showed you is how I would leverage the concept of a Relevancy Pyramid for a national SEO campaign.

Now let me show you how you can use this technique on the local level to prioritize link opportunities.

Local Relevancy Pyramid

Geo-targeted backlinks are the Creme de la creme of local SEO. That's why you must prioritize these opportunities in the Pyramid.

Here's how our local Relevancy Pyramid looks:

For this example, I will use a Chicago limo company.

Tier One: 100% Geo-Targeted and Niche Relevant

Your most prized prospects will be assigned here. That's because they must be both niche-relevant and geo-targeted relevant.

These are rare, but valuable.

An example would be a Chicago limo directory.

Tier Two: 100% Niche Relevant

Tier Two and Tier Three are interchangeable, but we like to focus on niche relevant links first.

Limos blogs, limo directories, and limo associations would fall under this category.

Tier Three: 100% Geo-Targeted

On Tier Three you would focus your efforts on Chicago-targeted opportunities.

Chicago directories and Chicago blogs are all fair game here.

Tier Four: 50% Niche Relevant

At this stage you would focus your efforts on related niches. Wedding blogs and wedding directories would fit into this category.

Tier Five: 25% Niche Relevant

On Tier Five you would focus on travel blogs, transportation blogs, and even dating blogs.

Here's how the local Relevancy Pyramid would look in

practice: I think you get it:

Link relevancy is super important, but how do you know if an opportunity is relevant?

You want to examine:

1. The general content "theme" of the linking domain. Is it relevant to yours?
2. The relevancy of the backlinks hitting the domain. The website linking to their website relevant to yours?

I recommend using Majestic's Topical Trust Flow Topics for this purpose.

2. Authority

The stronger the site, the better the results.

Since Google doesn't update PageRank anymore, you have to rely on third party metrics.

None of these third party tools are perfect, but they will do the

job. I recommend you analyze opportunities using all available

options. The best link analysis tools are:

- Ahrefs
- Majestic
- Open Site Explorer

3. Link Quality

Third party metrics such as Domain Rating (Ahrefs), Trust Flow (Majestic), and Domain Authority (Moz) can all be manipulated.

So, although a website can appear to be "authoritative" on the surface, it be outright dangerous when you dig deeper.

That's why you must examine the link profile of your

opportunities. All the tools I mentioned above will do the job.

Use these same standards I've outlined in this section to determine whether your link opportunity's link profile is high-quality or not.

4. Traffic

If you approach link acquisition with the intention of driving traffic to your website, it changes your entire mindset.

Your goal should be to get backlinks on website with real traffic.

This doesn't mean you'll get loads of referral traffic, but it's a good standard to have.

Since you will never know the exact traffic data of a site without getting in their analytics, you will need to use SEM Rush or Ahrefs.

5. Editorial Standards

Why are diamonds valuable? Because they're difficult to get. That's how you need to approach your link building. The harder it is to land a backlink, the more valuable it probably is.

On the other hand:

The easier a backlink is to get, the less valuable it is.

Focus on getting backlinks on websites that have editorial standards.

6. Outbound Link Quality

Websites with strong editorial guidelines will likely only link out to quality resources. You want your link to "live" around other quality outbound links.

Examine every prospective website and ask:

- What are they linking out to?
- Are the outbound links relevant?
- Are the outbound links going to respected, trusted sites?
- Do the outbound links look natural or do they look like paid links?

7. Indexation

This is by far the most obvious point, but the target website needs to be indexed in Google. If the site isn't indexed, then your backlinks will be worthless.

Just go to Google and search "site:example.com". If they don't show up, avoid the website.

You now know what a squeaky clean link profile looks like.

But now let me show you the backlinks you need to avoid.

Harmful Backlinks to AVOID

There are certain backlinks that should never touch your site.

If you decide to use these backlinks, just know that your risk for a penalty is much greater.

In fact:

I've seen websites get penalties for using these backlinks.

I'm telling you that because I don't want you to think I'm guessing.

It is a FACT that these backlinks can land you a manual or algorithmic penalty.

(Almost) Everything That's Irrelevant

Your tier one should be a wall of relevancy surrounding your site. I said "almost" every link should be relevant because of the Relevancy Pyramid principle I outlined above.

Public Networks

You can go on almost any SEO forum and buy backlinks on public networks. These networks will often advertise their service as "private blog networks". But that's a lie.

Once you are advertising a network, it is no longer private.

Throughout Google's short history, it has gone out of its way to smash public networks. After that, they go out and destroy every website that is using these networks.

It's easy for Google to spot these networks because:

A) there are an excessive amount of outbound links (typically 25-50+) on the homepage: homepages on REAL websites don't have a ridiculous amount of outbound links on the homepage.

B) the outbound links are completely irrelevant to each other: there will be links going to gambling sites, SEO sites, fitness sites, etc. It doesn't make any sense.

C) the content for each post is thin (only 250-300 words) Google's Panda algorithm hates thin content.

D) you can run, but you can't hide: some networks will attempt to block Ahrefs and Majestic crawlers, but its actually a footprint. On the other hand, networks that don't block crawlers will likely get reported to Google because of an angry competitor. It's a lose-lose situation.

These are some of the cheapest backlinks you can buy. They are also the perfect recipe for landing a penalty.

Large amounts of outbound links + irrelevant links + outbound links going to "bad neighborhoods" (gambling, pharma, porn, etc.) = a toxic backlink

Remember backlink quality indicator #6?

You don't want your link to live in this environment.

I'll admit that sidebar and footer backlinks can work, but they're also risky.

Standalone links look like paid backlinks and you know how Google feels about those.

Vendors that sell these high authority backlinks are also selling them to other websites. Most of these website will be irrelevant to yours. That's because these vendors rarely turn down money.

As a reminder:

You don't want your link to live with irrelevant or "bad neighborhood" links.

One more important note about sidebar/footer backlinks:

These links are almost always site-wide links.

This can destroy your site if you are using a keyword-rich anchor

text. It will wreck your anchor text profile.

I know web designers, marketing companies, and web hosting companies love footer backlinks.

So, if you do decide to use them, I recommend you use branded anchor text.

There is one exception to this rule:

If you can manipulate the code so that your link only shows on the homepage (where most of a site authority resides).

If you are using WordPress, you can use this Restrict Widgets plugin.

Automated Backlinks

As a general rule of thumb, you should avoid automated link building tools on tier one.

Some of these softwares include GSA, Ultimate Demon, and SENuke.

These softwares leverage spammed platforms and will likely land your site a penalty.

Now that you know what links to avoid like the plague, here are foundational backlinks you should build:

How to Build "Foundational" Backlinks

"Foundational" backlinks are what every normal website should have.

They will create a layer of trust around your site.

That's because you will be using nothing but unoptimized, branded backlinks from authority sites.

We use this exact approach with every client we take on and it works extremely well.

Important note:

You should only use naked link or branded anchors for foundational backlinks.

The first thing you need to do is secure all your social media properties.

At the very minimum, your business should have:

- Facebook
- Twitter (follow me)
- LinkedIn (connect with
- me) Pinterest
- Instagram

You don't have to actively market on these platforms, but it certainly wouldn't hurt.

For example, for Gotch SEO, my social media manager decided that Facebook was our best social media platform based on referral traffic and engagement.

That's why we are "all-in" on Facebook and not as active on the other

platforms. Choose what platforms work best for your business.

At the minimum, populate these accounts and share some content, so that you at least have a base.

Business Listings/Citations

Google values business listings so much that it is apart of the local search algorithm.

This should be more than enough for you to use them for ANY SEO campaign.

The cool part about listings is that about 50% of them give you a Follow, unoptimized link.

Business citations are a perfect way to build a foundation of trust around your site.

Remember earlier when I said that not all backlinks hitting your site need to be 100% relevant?

I was referring to business listings and social media profiles.

Google trusts these platforms and is well aware that all types of businesses will be using them.

In a sense, they get a pass for not being relevant.

Niche-Targeted Directories

While most directories are pretty much worthless, there are some diamonds in the rough.

Niche-targeted directories offer both a relevant and Follow link.

As you know, backlinks with both of these characteristics are hard to come by.

Use these search strings in Google to find niche directories:

- NICHE + Directory (Example: "fitness + directory")
- NICHE directories
- NICHE + "submit site"

Geo-Targeted Directories

Geo-targeted directories are a must-have link source for local businesses.

Here are some search strings you can use to find geo-targeted

directories:

- city + directory
- directory + city
- submit my site +
  city
- niche + city +
- directory city +
  directories

I'm always amazed why so many SEOs skip out on niche relevant blog comments. Too many SEOs neglect them because of the dreaded "NoFollow" tag.

I highly recommend you don't neglect them.

My agency uses niche relevant blog comments to:

- A) create a layer of relevancy around our client's site
- B) improve to the ratio of Follow and NoFollow backlinks
- C) diversify our anchors in a meaningful way
- D) sometimes get small amounts of referral traffic

Back in 2013, I was the first person comment on one of Brian's article:

This one comment has sent my site 143 visitors since:

E)

build a relationship with the blogger that you could leverage for backlinks in the

future. Point "D" is the most important and where most SEOs mess up.

Don't go to a top blog and write a "me too" comment or something general/useless.

This doesn't build relationships.

You have to contribute to the blog in a meaningful

way. Most important:

You have to ADD VALUE.

This doesn't mean you need to write a five paragraph

essay. In fact, I advise against that.

Focus on one point and leave a concise, well-thought out comment.

Niche Relevant Forum Backlinks

Participating on industry forums is an excellent way to build brand recognition.

And if you do it right, you will drive some relevant referral traffic to your

website. Here is the traffic the BlackHatWorld.com has sent my site since

2014:

This is referral traffic coming from 18 different threads in the forum.

Forum members have linked to my content, but it wouldn't be hard to orchestrate it if you are creative.

There aren't many forums that allow signature backlinks, but many still allow profile backlinks. These profile backlinks are valuable because they are relevant and Follow in most cases.

To get the most out of your forum profile backlinks, I'm going to show you some quick techniques.

1. Prospect for relevant forums

Use the following search strings in Google to find forums:

- forum +
- NICHE
  NICHE +
  forum

2. Take time to fill out your profile

Since your link will likely be a naked link, you need to leverage co-occurrence.

Co-occurrence is when your website's target keyword phrase is near to your link.

Just write a legitimate profile description and make sure to toss in your main keyword.

3. Understand the forum "personality" / etiquette

Every forum is different and you need to learn how each operates.

Some tolerate a little self-promotion while others will ban you for it.

Scan through the forum and see if members are sharing links in

threads.

4. Increase your post count & start adding friends

The more posts/friends you have, the more trust you build on the forum. Also, more connections send more internal links back to your profile page.

This will slowly build the authority of your profile page.

5. Start a thread

Starting well-thought-out threads is a great way to build credibility on the forum.

Okay, now you might be asking what's the point of doing all this?

The goal is to increase the amount of internal links hitting your profile page.

This leverages the forums authority. As a result it will increase the authority of your profile page hosting your link.

The second goal of all this work is so you can become a part of the forum community and so that members trust you more.

If you have a good reputation on the forum, you can share your content without getting flamed or banned.

You now know what it takes to build a solid foundation of backlinks. Now it's time to get into what I like to call "Power" backlinks.

Power Backlinks

"Power" backlinks will accelerate your results because:

A) they are the most relevant and

B) they are the most authoritative

Content-Driven Approach

As hard as it is to produce quality content, there is no better way to drive high authority backlinks to a website.

There are only three things you have to do with a content-driven approach:

1. Find the right keywords to target
2. Create a great piece of content around that keyword
3. Promote the content (social and backlinks)

When you create quality content, you are creating ASSETS for your business.

No matter what Google does, it can never take away your content.

You need to approach link building with a long-term mindset in 2020 and

beyond. I use the investing analogy pretty often, but it's true for SEO.

There is a compound effect of producing and promoting content on a consistent basis.

Keep in mind:

The following tactics are effective without content.

But you will get even better results if you build links to strong content assets.

Editorial Backlinks

For a link to be "editorial" you can't have access to the site and your link must pass editorial review. Google values editorial backlinks more than any other type of link.

Sadly, getting these high authority backlinks can be challenging.

First, you have to build relationships with bloggers in your industry. Second, you likely need to produce quality content to get natural backlinks.

My agency has acquired thousands of high-quality editorial backlinks at this point. We can get these high authority backlinks because we have built relationships and have the connections.

Also:

Don't forget to leverage any existing assets you already have. For example, I reviewed Death Wish Coffee on The Darkest Roast and it needs backlinks to rank well. The quickest win is to leverage any existing asset I already have.

See what I did there?

Notice that I placed my primary keyword phrase in close proximity to link. This is safer than using a keyword-rich anchor in this instance because Gotch SEO isn't relevant to The Darkest Roast.

Niche Relevant Guest Posts

Guest posts are effective in two ways.

- First, if you contribute lots of value, it will build your authority in the space.
- Second, your guest post can send relevant referral traffic to your website.

Keep in mind that Google frowns upon spammy guest posting. That means you need to focus your efforts on producing a valuable guest post. If you give value, then there is nothing wrong with injecting backlinks to your website.

To get the most out of your guest posts, you need to get contextual links. Contextual links are far more powerful than author byline links.

Here are some search queries to find opportunities:

NICHE + "guest post"
NICHE + "contribute
to" NICHE + "write for
us" NICHE +
"contributors" NICHE
+ "guest writer"
NICHE + "guest post guidelines"

The Merger Technique

The Merger Technique is the process of finding a relevant expired domain and 301 redirecting it to your site.

The concept is simple:

You just acquired a relevant business and want to redirect to your mother company. The key is for the expired domain to be 100% relevant.

These domains are harder to come by, but it is well worth it when you find one.

Resource Pages

This is an oldie, but a goodie.

Although SEO's have abused this strategy, there are still some diamonds in the rough.

Once you find the pages, it's best to see if there are any broken links on the page.

Use the Check My Link plugin.

You can use this as leverage when reaching out.

If there are no broken links, then you will need a strong content asset.

Otherwise, you'll likely get denied.

The White Alternative to PBNs

The White Hat Alternative to PBNs is simple:

Instead of buying an expired domain and rebuilding it, you are going to:

1. find an expired domain
2. scrape its backlinks
3. then reach out and let the linkers know they are linking to a dead resource

If the expired domain is relevant, you can ask the linker to replace the dead link with your site.

To improve your success rate, suggest 2-3 quality resources (including yours).

You can also recreate the original content if it's relevant. This is obvious, but the content must better than the original.

Reach out and let the linker know about the new, revised piece of content.

This strategy requires more time and effort, but you get more link placements.

Read more about the strategy here.

Grey Hat Backlinks

I stay away from grey hat techniques at this point, but I did live in this world for a long time.

NOTE: if you take the grey hat route, you are increasing the likelihood of getting a penalty.

None of these tactics are safe and I have seen websites get manual penalties using each of them.

If there is so much risk, then why am I showing you?

The reason is because many of these techniques work

well. These techniques are best for people:

- Who have a high risk tolerance
- Who want to rank without creating great
- content Who don't care if their site gets penalized

If you have a low risk tolerance then you have two options:

A) avoid these backlinks altogether or B) use them on tier two to boost your tier one backlinks.

Leverage Relevant Expired Domains

If you are going to create a PBN, then you might as well do it

right. Don't just buy any expired domain.

Try to find domains that have relevant Topical Trust Flow Topics to your niche.

This won't always be possible, but it's worth the patience.

Getting a link from one relevant domain is more powerful than several irrelevant domains.

Here are my favorite tools for finding expired domains:

- Freshdrop
- DomCop

Here's how you can use DomCop to find expired domains:

Some other options include: ExpiredDomains.net and Moonsy.

Web 2.0s

Creating web 2.0s on sites like Tumblr, Weebly, and WordPress.com is an old grey hat strategy that still works. Just be careful because it can land you a penalty. I have gotten manual actions removed from clients because of web 2.0 backlinks.

I recommend you avoid using these backlinks on tier one.

Read The Art of The Super Web 2.0 to learn how to build them correctly.

How to EARN Backlinks

Many people doing SEO confuse earning backlinks with building backlinks.

These are two different concepts.

To EARN, means that you DESERVE backlinks.

Have you ever taken a second to think about why your website even deserves backlinks?

I've realized that there is only one way to EARN backlinks...

You must become obsessed with pleasing your users.

As of late, I have become consumed with the overwhelming ambition to please my users.

After hours of thought, I've realized that effective SEO starts with the user in mind.

You have to be user-centric.

If you please the user, you will please Google.

I used to spend so much of my time trying to figure out how to "trick" or manipulate Google.

I can't get that time back, but I have learned an important

lesson: To build a real business, you must focus on pleasing the

user.

All the time. On a consistent basis.

Understand that:

- Happy users ARE your marketing.
- Happy users will EARN you
  backlinks.
- Happy users will SHARE your content on social
- media. Happy users will RETURN to your website.

Your SEO campaign will transform when you put your users first.

Let me show you how to earn backlinks by being user-centric:

11 Ways to Earn Backlinks

1. You Have to Become User-Centric

Let's face it:

If users don't like your website, then Google won't either.

Your focus shouldn't be on manipulating algorithms.

Your focus should be "what can I do right now to help my prospective customers or readers?"

There isn't a single website online that can't improve User Experience

(UX). There is always room to help more and give more.

A website that puts 100% effort into pleasing the user, will earn

backlinks. You need to remember how Google interprets a backlink.

It is a vote. Some of these "votes" are better than others.

Think off it this way:

The U.S. just went through an election cycle.

Candidates from the Republicans and Democrats are battling to earn their
party's nomination.

When you cut through all the media noise there is a powerful marketing technique at
play:

Endorsements.

Whenever a candidate gets an endorsement from a well-known figure in the party, it
is a huge deal.

A single endorsement can get enormous amounts of news coverage.

Here are two examples:

Google Trends After Sarah Palin Endorsed Donald Trump

Google Trends After Glenn Beck Endorsed Ted Cruz

Look at those spikes immediately following

endorsements. Think of backlinks as endorsements for

your website.

What does your site/blog have to deserve a big endorsement?

Small endorsements are fine and will compound overtime.

But getting an endorsement from a well-known site in your industry is way more powerful.

The only way to get such endorsements (backlinks), you need to give tremendous value for the user.

2. Your Content Must Please the User

You know how competitive content marketing is in the entrepreneur, SEO, and marketing industries.

Bloggers are pumping out incredible pieces of content.

Sometimes these content pieces are more than 10,000 words.

Others times, hundreds of hours are investing doing research and finding data.

This is the standard in these industries.

Yet, this isn't the standard in every industry.

Should it be?

Maybe.

But it's not.

There isn't a single formula for creating content that pleases a user.

That's why it can be dangerous immersing yourself in the industries

above. It narrows your view.

You start to think that "good" content has to be 1,800 words or more.

The truth is:

"Good" content comes in all shapes and

sizes. There are no laws for creating great

content.

I do not believe that every piece of content you create needs to rank on the first page of Google.

Yes, most of your content should focus on a single keyword.

But, don't let the search engine determine what types of content you want to produce.

There are times when you need to solve a micro problem in your content.

This micro problem may only get 10 searches a month in Google.

WHO CARES.

As long as you have the intention of helping someone, it will improve the value of your website.

There isn't a problem too big or too small.

SEOs get wrapped up in data, but forget about the user.

Who cares if Google is telling you that a particular keyword only gets 10 searches a month.

For all I care, that is an opportunity to help approximately 10 people.

You want to know what's funny?

When I created the article "How to Index Backlinks 100% of the Time", there wasn't any search volume.

I didn't care that it didn't have search volume at the time.

I just knew it was a problem because I was the one struggling with it!

I spent a few hours created that content and it's driven **111,000 pageviews** from **Organic Search** this year alone:

The moral of the story is that your content needs to help people reach a goal or solve a problem.

It doesn't always need to be monumental.

- Creating something that makes someone laugh is solving a
- problem. Showing someone how to sharpen a pencil is solving a problem.
- Telling someone about the mistakes you've made helps them avoid those mistakes.

You get the point.

Focus on the user

first.

What are their problems and what can you do to help them?

After you figure that out, then you need to make sure that…

3. Your Content Stand Outs

Creating rehashed garbage won't get you anywhere. It won't help you in Google and it won't help your business grow.

The successful businesses we see in the world are

innovative. They don't think about how to copy their

competitors.

They think about what they can do that's different and unique.

Take a look at the pages ranking in Google for your target

keyword.

Think: "What can I do that's different than these 10 pages?"

Here are the common characteristics/quality holes you want to look

for: Outdated Content

Creating updated content is the single biggest way to be

different. Time is the enemy of many blogs.

Not all content will become outdated if it's

evergreen. But, it depends on the industry.

For example, the SEO industry changes at a rapid pace.

Marketing in general is always changing and there are always new mediums emerging.

Content gets outdated.

When you find outdated content, there's opportunity.

The most obvious plan of attack is to create an updated piece of content, but that's not all:

You must create an updated piece of content that blows the other one out of the water.

Don't play nice when it comes to helping the user.

It is a competition to see who can help the user more.

You need to win.

Lack of Depth

Sometimes it's mind boggling why some pages even rank on the first page of Google.

Many times, these pages are ranking because their site has so much authority.

If a page is ranking because of its site authority, it's an opportunity for you.

Pages that rank in this fashion will likely have "thin" content. You can dominate them by creating content with more depth. Not just a little more depth. Create massive depth in your content.

Like I said above, don't let it be a competition.

Your content should be so good that your competitors don't even attempt to beat it.

Lack of Data or Research

Some content ranking on the first page of Google is great, but lacks data and

research. If you identify pages like this, you can overwhelm them with data and

research.

Leverage trusted data sources in your industry.

If there isn't lots of data available on hand, then create your own case studies.

These case studies will give you unique data that will make your content stand out.

Lack of Personality

Some content on the first page of Google will put you to sleep. The content has a "corporate", impersonal tone.

Content becomes "corporate" when the company loses sight of the user.

They become out of touch.

Great content and copywriting is suppose to be simple and personal.

Beating corporate speak is my goal with Gotch SEO.

When I see content that's ranking well (without personality), I know I will smash

them. I do my best to speak to YOU.

I want YOU to know that I'm helping

YOU. YOU are what matters.

YOU are the reason why I even produce content.

Use "YOU" in your content.

Speak to your reader.

You aren't writing for an audience.

You are writing for a single

individual.

Do me a favor:

I want you to "LOL" next time you see a page ranking with "corporate", impersonal content.

Why?

Because it's your job to push them off the first page of Google by being personal and caring more about your users.

Lack of Readability & Visual
Appeal I'm sure you have seen
it:

- unbearable big blocks of
- text no headings
- no images
- white font on a black
- backgrounds distracting designs

As I mentioned above, there are pages that rank because of their website's authority.

Some of these pages will have essay-like content that gives me college flashbacks.

To beat them, create content that:

- is readable (use bullet points, lists,
- etc.) is easy to scan (use descriptive headings)
- uses beautiful visuals.(use images to break up long content)
- has black font on a white background (it's easier to read/a proven copywriting principle)
- doesn't have distracting design elements. (your content is the most important element on the page. Don't let your design take away from.)

4. You Must Be Willing to Do What Others Won't

You have likely noticed a trend in this article already. Great content marketing AND ranking pages in Google requires enormous amounts of effort. You have to be willing to do what others won't.

The good news is that most people are lazy.

- It's hard to sit down and write every single day.
- It's hard to think outside of the box.
- It's hard not to get distracted.

But that's what it takes if you want to create content that produces results.

You aren't always going to get it right, but the more you produce, the better chance you have to succeed.

Produce. Produce. Produce.

And when you finish producing, start producing more.

5. You Must Be Creative

Being creative is hard, but everyone struggles with coming up with unique ideas.

Many of your ideas will likely suck, but it doesn't matter. You only need a few good ideas to stick to start seeing growth.

Creative content will attract high authority backlinks.

At the same time, don't feel like you need to always reinvent the wheel.

Brian talks about this a lot, but you should look at content that has performed well in the past.

Use tools like Buzzsumo and the first page of Google to see what content has attracted the most backlinks.

You can then use the same idea, but create something completely unique and better.

Keep im mind:

This is still creativity!

The only difference is that you aren't coming up with ideas out of thin are.

Instead, you are using ideas that are already validated. This will increase your content's chances of success.

6. You Need to Be Unique

I can't stand rehashed information. I see it so often across all verticals and it's painful to see.

Rehashed content won't earn you backlinks.

If all you can think of are rehashed ideas, then don't publish at all.

It's better to publish one super unique piece of content than it is to produce rehashed garbage.

Make it unique.

Be creative and be different.

Bloggers link to content that is innovative, unique, and super valuable.

7. You Must Outperform Others

As I explained in a previous step, you need to beat your competitors.

There are likely a few competitors in your industry that are producing stellar

content. You need to outperform them.

They are the benchmark.

Analyze their content and do your best to understand why it performs well.

Ask:

- WHY do they get so many social
- shares? WHY do they get so many blog comments?
- What makes them different from the thousands of other bloggers in your industry?

Understanding why they are successful will help you develop a plan to beat them.

Remember:

The goal isn't to beat them in a slimy or unethical way.

The goal is to beat them by giving MORE value.

That needs to be your goal no matter how hard it may be.

8. You Have to Be Consistent

Instead of trying to be perfect, you need to be

consistent. You should try to produce at least some

content everyday. Will it always be a masterpiece?

No.

It's the ACT of producing content is what's actually valuable. That's because your efforts will compound overtime.

It's about putting hard work day-in and day-out.

You can look at Derek's blog and see that he only publishes 1-2 times a month.

Does that mean he's chillen' the rest of the month?

NO.

He's working on other parts of his business that will bring value to his readers. It doesn't matter how often you publish. It matters that you are producing value on a daily basis.

The more you produce, the better you will become.

Your thoughts will crystallize.

It's obvious when someone worked super hard to produce a piece of content. That's because the more effort you put into a piece of content, the better it will be.

The better content is, the more backlinks you will attract.

But you HAVE to be consistent.

Consistency isn't some God-given talent. It's about organization and planning.

That's why you should consider using an editorial calendar.

Editorial calendar help end decision fatigue. You will wake up and know what needs to get done without having to think about it.

You want your content production to be on auto-pilot.

Here are resources for creating an editorial calendar:

- How To Boost Success With A Content Marketing Editorial
- Calendar A Content Marketer's Checklist: Editorial Calendar Essentials
- 10 Reasons Your Editorial Calendar Sucks (and How to Make It the Best)

9. You Have to Build Relationships

To earn backlinks, you need to build relationships. Your blog can't be an island in the middle of the ocean. You need build connections and relationships.

These relationships will lead to backlinks. You won't even have to ask for a link most of the time.

Just the act of establishing relationships with top bloggers will often lead to links.

That is, as long as your content is valuable and unique.

When trying to build relationships, you need to always focus on what YOU can do for the person.

Do you remember what I said about being user-centric?

The same principle applies when trying to build relationships. You should be thinking about how you can help the prospect. Not how you can get more out of them.

Give, give, and give more. Then, you will receive.

Think about it:

Why would anyone want to link to your blog after getting a cold email request? I know I wouldn't.

To get your blog and name "out there" you need to use

repetition. That means your name needs to visible on many

fronts.

Start with a well-thought-out comment on their blog. Then follow that up with a Tweet or response to a Tweet of theirs. Then send them a non-committal email.

Repeat this cycle over and over until it's obvious that they know your name.

Once you have gone through this effort, THEN ask them how you can help them in one way or another.

How can you give them value? Why should they link to your content?

Does your content deserve links from a top blog? Is it THAT good?

You will always have a biased answer.

That's why you should seek outside opinions. ASK top bloggers what they think about your content.

(Asking bloggers "what they think" about your content is a great way to get exposure).

10. You Need to Build an Email List

That's right.

One of the best ways to earn backlinks is to have an email list. That's because you can email your list whenever you publish a new blog post. The people on your list are receptive to you and like what you are doing.

Many of these same subscribers also have blogs of their own.

It is much more likely that a loyal subscriber will link to your content than it happening at random.

I'm sure you have seen this happen:

A top blogger publishes a new blog post and BAM:

They have countless social shares and comments within

hours. How does this happen?

It's because they promote their content to their list! Having an email list is a true asset for your business. You have complete control of your email list.

- It isn't affected by algorithm
- changes. It isn't affected by policy changes.
- It's yours and it's the ultimate asset.

Growing an email list should be a priority for EVERY business.

ProoTTiip: It's important to note that your email list is only valuable if your emails actually reach your subscriber's inbox. Otherwise, they won't be opened. Fortunately, free tools like MailGenius help make sure your emails get delivered (and opened) instead of landing in the spam folder.

11. You Need to Promote Your Content

Yes, to EARN backlinks, people must see your content.

Invisible content doesn't get backlinks, no matter how good it is.

Content promotion is a topic I'll be explaining in future posts because it's comprehensive.

But here's a simple technique you can use:

Similar Content Outreach

This is one of my favorite tactics. Here's how to do it:

The most important element of this strategy is to have a great piece of content. It needs to be much better than the other relevant piece of content they are linking to.

To find prospects use Buzzsumo or look at the first page of Google for your target keyword.

Take the top 10 results and run them through Ahrefs or Majestic.

Also:

Make sure you avoid cold outreach. I haven't gone too deep into outreach here, but make sure you warm your prospects up before hitting them with a pitch.

Trust me:

Only a micro percentage of people will link to your blog after getting a cold email request.

They may not change links, but they might link to your resource in a future article. If they don't link, then they will likely share the content piece on social.

Also, remember to share your content on your owned media assets such as Facebook, Twitter, etc. It's important to engage with the audience you already have because it can lead to natural links.

Bonus: What About Guest Posting?

I'm a big fan of guest posting, but it's not a way to EARN backlinks for your website.

The reason is because you are the one responsible for placing the link back to your site.

That isn't earned.

In essence, YOU are deciding that your website or content is worth linking to.

EARNED means that you created a great piece of content, promoted it, and someone linked to it by free will.

Like I said, there is nothing wrong with guest posting for:

- brand building
- traffic generation
- link building

But as far as being an EARNED backlink, it is

not. If you control the link, it's not earned.

Still have some questions about backlinks?

Frequently Asked Questions About Backlinks

My backlinks are decreasing. What now?

It's natural and normal to lose some links overtime. That's why it's critical to remember that link acquisition isn't a one time event. It needs to be an on-going activity. You should always be taking actions to acquire new backlinks to make up for those that you lose.

My backlinks are not showing in Google Search Console, Ahrefs, etc. Why?

Google Search Console only shows a sample of your total link profile. While third party tools like Ahrefs are amazing at find backlinks, they aren't perfect or comprehensive. Assume that these tools are only showing a percentage of your entire link profile.

Are backlinks still important?

Other factors such as content quality and User Experience (UX) have become more prominent, but backlinks are still super important for ranking. You can rank for some uncompetitive keywords if your website is authoritative. However, in most scenarios, you'll need high-quality backlinks to give you that final push.

Are Fiverr backlinks good?

In my experience, 99% of link opportunities on Fiverr are bad. In general, I would avoid buying backlinks from Fiverr. Remember… you usually get what you pay for.

Are NoFollow backlinks good?

NoFollow backlinks are not good or effective because they don't pass PageRank. The only time they're useful is if you're getting referral traffic or sales. But from an SEO perspective, they have no value.

How many backlinks do I need?

Grab your target keyword and open up Ahrefs Keyword Explorer tool. Scroll down and export the top 10 results for your target keyword phrase. Then, average out the total linking root domains for these results. That average is a good target for how many backlinks you'll need to rank.

How many backlinks per day is safe?

You only need to worry about link velocity when you're building artificial backlinks. If you're acquiring backlinks through outreach and content promotion, then you don't need to worry about this.

How many backlinks do I have?

Go Ahrefs, Majestic, SEMRush, or Open Site Explorer and they'll give you an idea of how many total backlinks you have. Ahrefs is the most comprehensive (IMO).

That's a Wrap!

The art of acquiring backlinks is a massive topic, but I hoped this gave you the right framework for acquiring more.

Thanks for reading!

www.ingramcontent.com/pod-product-compliance
Lightning Source LLC
Chambersburg PA
CBHW080532060326
40690CB00022B/5100